Wines from the Countryside

Wines from the Countryside

with beer, mead, cider and other drinks for good measure

Ben Turner

B. T. BATSFORD LTD
London

Dedication

We have this wine to offer
    fruit of the earth and work of human hands
Thank you Lord
    for all your Blessings

ISBN 0 7134 4110 0 (cased)

Typeset by Deltatype, Ellesmere Port
and printed in Great Britain by
R. J. Acford
Chichester, Sussex
for the publishers
B. T. Batsford Ltd
4 Fitzhardinge Street
London W1H 0AH

Contents

Preface

In August 1945 my great-aunt, Jane Gould, who was even then over 70 years of age, showed me how to make wine from the wild blackberries that my wife and I had collected from the hedgerows. It was a good year, for the wine was delicious and I was quickly hooked onto a new hobby. Although sugar was rationed in those post-war days, I made wine whenever I could and have continued to do so ever since. For many years now I have been making between 60 and 100 gallons a year, and I drink some wine every day. I have 'experimented' with most available fruits, flowers, vegetables and other ingredients, especially if they were for free from the countryside!

Although I have written many books on different aspects of this ever-growing hobby, I have not previously written exclusively about the true country wines, meads, beers and ciders. Nowadays, many people use concentrated fruit compounds from which to make their different wine styles. The method is clean and simple and the wine is quickly ready for drinking. Kit wines are very good if you like them, and millions of people do.

Another group of people could well be called 'amateur winemakers' for they blend different ingredients together in an endeavour to produce wines similar in style to commercial wines. Some of these wines are of outstanding quality and are well worth the extra trouble. They have a complex vinous bouquet and flavour and it is usually impossible to guess from what ingredients they were made.

The country winemaker, on the other hand, mostly makes wine from a single base ingredient and is proud that the finished product possesses the fragrance and flavour of the fruits, flowers, vegetables or herbs that have been used. Because of strong ingredient flavour, many of these wines usually taste best when served with a sweet finish. Those people who are not accustomed to drinking wine often prefer a sweetish wine and so frequently enjoy these country wines in preference to others.

Preface

In this book I want to show those who are new to the hobby of making alcoholic drinks in the home not only how to make enjoyable country wines, meads, ciders and beers, but also how to make at least some of these drinks in a more sophisticated manner suitable for enjoying with meals. The inclusion of a small quantity of sultanas (or grapes in any other form), adjustment of the acid and sugar quantities, and the use of specific wine yeasts are the main differences.

If you enjoy fresh, natural foods in preference to the 'convenience' foods so often prepared in a factory, then you will enjoy these natural beverages made from fresh ingredients and prepared by yourself, so that you know exactly what is in them. Only the barest minimum of chemical additives are recommended and then, like pectolytic enzyme and sulphite, only if they enhance the quality of the wines and protect them from evil.

This book offers no gimmicks of instant wine, only commonsense advice in the use of ingredients from the countryside to make alcoholic drinks. The advice is given in plain and easy-to-read language so that it can be followed without difficulty. The different ingredients are each described in some detail so as to increase your appreciation and enjoyment of the wines made from them.

If you pay me the courtesy of reading the advice before you start, I promise that you will make better beverages from the recipes. The 'secret' of good home winemaking and brewing is a clear understanding of what you are doing, coupled with cleanliness and patience. I will help you with the first if you will provide the other two. The result can only be 'Good Health'!

1 Historical introduction

In the history of alcoholic beverages country wines are relatively new. Country wines have to be made with sugar and this ingredient was not widely available until the latter half of the seventeenth century. Although sugar was known some 500 years before the Birth of Christ, and was imported into England as early as 1264, it was extremely expensive, and remained so until the colonisation of the West Indies and the production of cheap sugar by slave labour from the sugar cane plant.

Until that time honey was the only ingredient that could be used for sweetening. Many different fruits, flowers and herbs were used to flavour solutions of honey in the making of meads, but the resulting beverages were melomels rather than country wines as we now know them.

In 1635 King Charles I granted permission to Francis Chamberlayne to make and sell wines from 'raysons' and other fruits of the realm. He was successful and others, no doubt, also began to ferment fruit juices.

By 1675 quite a number of books had been published giving advice on how to make wines from fruits, how to rack and fine them, how to make imitations of imported wines from France, even how to blend imported grape wines with home-produced fruit wines and market them as superior wines!

The craft of making fruit wines naturally developed in the small villages. Most of the wines were made by the women, who also baked and who were therefore familiar with yeast and sugar. Because of their relative poverty, as well as their distance from doctors, the women often included medicinal herbs in their wines. These wines were thought of as a remedy for a wide range of illnesses or complaints. At any rate, some country wines acquired a reputation for being beneficial in certain circumstances. At that time cowslip, dandelion and elderflower wines were among the most popular in this connection, with elderberry close behind.

The wines were undoubtedly very sweet and, unless they had been laced with brandy, unlikely to have been very strong, although the alleged potency of parsnip wine, for example, endured until the 1960s. Most of them would be lacking acid in spite of the addition of the occasional orange or lemon. It is likely, too, that a good number would be cloudy and, however many were drinkable, it is probable that many had to be thrown away. Hygiene, as we understand it, with an awareness of the risk of infection from invisible micro-organisms, hardly existed.

Fruits were left steeping in water for two or three weeks, covered only by a muslin cloth. A fine selection of moulds would surely have settled on the surface. Wild yeasts can only ferment sugar to four per cent of alcohol. This is the ideal amount for bacteria to convert into vinegar!

Nevertheless, sufficient palatable wines were made to encourage further making. As today, some people had a better flair for winemaking than others. Fruit, flower, vegetable and herb wines were made not only in the country cottages but also in the splendid houses of the country squire and well-to-do farmers. Here a room would be set aside for the making, fermenting and maturing of wines, ciders, meads, ales and spirits. The facilities in these houses usually included a small still, called an alembic. It was used for making liqueurs, ratafias (a beverage usually made by adding fruit juice and other flavourings, and sugar, to spirit) and cordials from flowers as well as fruits. We now know that drinking imperfectly distilled spirits can cause stomach upsets, and, in severe cases, blindness and even death, and Parliament has sensibly forbidden home distillation, whether by heating or freezing.

With the great move to the towns for employment during the Industrial Revolution, home winemaking began to decline. New beverages were available, notably tea, and for those who needed quick relief from the trauma of existence, gin, the drink that soon became known as 'mother's ruin'. It was said that you could become drunk for a penny and dead drunk for twopence.

The shortages of sugar during and after the First World War from 1914 to 1918, so soon followed by the Second World War from 1939 to 1945, reduced winemaking in the countryside to minute proportions. But in 1945 interest suddenly awakened in the towns. Returning servicemen who had developed a taste for wine in Europe, and the great expansion of holidays abroad, stimulated the infant movement. In 1954 a small group of winemakers in Andover formed an association and arranged to meet once a month to exchange ideas and taste each others' wines. Similar associations were being formed in Welwyn Garden City and other small towns in the Home Counties.

The first books giving advice and recipes to the new winemakers appeared and a monthly magazine was published. The first gathering of winemakers from different circles and a competition of wines their members had made was held in 1959. A National Association of Winemakers was formed in 1961 and a great gathering has been held every year but one, in some suitable conference centre that can cater for a thousand or more winemakers and their four thousand bottles of wine.

In 1963 a small Guild of Wine Judges was formed, and since 1964 has only admitted new members after they have passed an examination of competency. Membership has now grown to nearly 300 and includes those competent to adjudicate on beer, mead and cider.

In the late 1960s cans of concentrated grape juice were marketed. Flavourings had been added to produce wines similar in style to commercial wine. All that was needed was water, some extra sugar and yeast. Eventually, a great range of more than twenty different types of wine was developed. The number of manufacturers increased, and the competition resulted in an improvement in the quality of the wines produced. Several million people regularly make wine from these kits.

Towards the end of the 1950s and in the early 1960s, it became possible to buy specific wine yeasts as opposed to baker's yeast and brewer's yeast. With the growth in plastics came purpose-designed equipment for the winemakers, such as polythene bins, funnels and siphons, hydrometers and trial jars, fermentation jars and airlocks, nylon straining bags, small presses, filter kits, etc. A wide range of long-lasting equipment is now available, for the craft of making wine at home is big business and it looks as though this hobby is set for continued growth.

2 Equipment for winemaking

The quantity and variety of equipment needed for making wine in the home naturally depends on how much wine you make. If you have already made some wine you will, no doubt, already have the basic equipment. If you are new to winemaking then buy only the essential equipment at first and increase your range as you progress.

Many home brew shops and centres sell a **Beginner's Kit**. Generally they include a food grade, natural polythene bin and lid, a length of plastic tubing, a glass demijohn and bung, a bored cork and airlock, a polythene funnel, a can of concentrated grape juice and a sachet of yeast, a few Campden tablets and, maybe, six corks or labels. All that you will need to provide to make your first gallon of wine is a few pints of cold water, a small quantity of sugar and six empty wine bottles. Some kits include the bottles and omit the bin. But the bin is very important. It can be used for mixing up the must, for receiving the young wine when racking and for fermenting fruit wines on the pulp. It also makes a good storage container for small equipment when not in use.

Bins are available in a variety of sizes and finishes. The basic sizes are 10, 15 and 25 litres (2¼, 3⅓ and 5½ gallons.) Many have graduated quantity markings on the side, a few have taps close to the bottom of the bin and/or a grommet in the lid for the fitting of a bored bung and airlock.

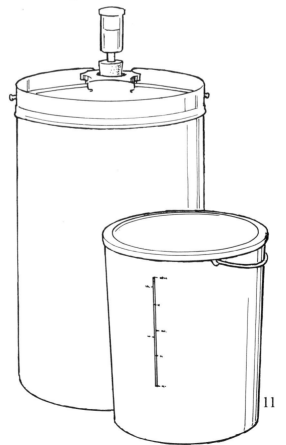

11

Equipment for winemaking

Demijohns with a nominal capacity of one gallon are also needed. Several, really, are required for they are frequently used for storing the wine for several months while it matures. The possession of only one such jar prevents the making of a second wine until the first is bottled. Once you get started you will soon find good use for quite a number of demijohns.

The ideal storage container for small quantities of wine is made from glazed earthenware and available in 5- and 10-litre sizes. These jars are heavy and you cannot see the wine inside them, but they are so thick that they insulate the wine from sudden changes of temperature and also keep out the light.

There is much stirring to be done in the many different aspects of home brew and for this purpose a **plastic spoon** or paddle is needed. A **wooden spoon** will do almost as well, but the wood is more difficult to sterilise than a plastic spoon.

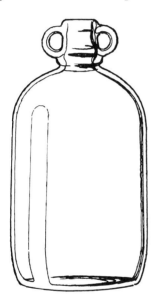

Small and large polythene **funnels** always have uses. Buy those with some ridges around the outside of the tube so that air can escape from the vessel as it is being filled. Otherwise large bubbles of air force their way up through the liquid in the funnel and burst with a splattering mess.

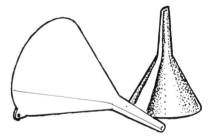

Bored bungs, made either from cork or rubber, are needed together with one or two **airlocks**. These are made from glass or plastic and one end fits tightly into the hole in the centre of the bung. A small quantity of sulphite solution poured into the device acts as the lock that keeps out the air whilst permitting the fermentation gas to escape.

Solid bungs are needed for sealing the jars during storage. Alternatively, you can use a **safety bung** that seals the jar effectively, but contains a facility for allowing the gas from any subsequent fermentation to escape.

A long-handled **bottle brush** is essential for cleaning the punts and shoulders of bottles and jars. Some yeast and tartrate deposits can be very difficult to move without the aid of a brush.

Siphons are available in a variety of forms ranging from a simple piece of plastic tubing to one with a J tube at the end, a tap at the other and a small hand pump in the middle. As an alternative to the J tube that sucks the wine down, one can buy a tube that has a sealed end and several holes in the side so that the wine is drawn in across the surface of the sediment. Plastic is hard to squeeze adequately between finger and thumb, hence the need for a tap or a laboratory clip. Alternatively, a very short length of rubber tubing could be fitted on to the plastic since the rubber is much easier to seal with a finger squeeze.

Proper **wine bottles** are essential. Spirit bottles and their screw caps may well be too thin if a post-bottling fermentation should occur. The bottle may burst with disastrous results, especially in warm weather and at a time when the bottle is being moved. Screw-stoppered mineral water, sauce or similar bottles diminish the aesthetic appeal of a

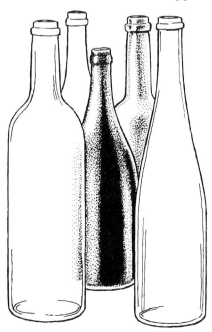

wine. Wine bottles may be bought but can often be obtained free from licensed restaurants and hotels. Soak them in warm water to remove all the old labels and thoroughly wash the bottles inside and out; rinse them in clean cold water, then sterilise them and drain them before use.

Wine bottles need long **cylindrical corks** to seal them and a tool for inserting the corks into the bottles. These **corking tools** come in a variety of shapes from the wooden cylinder and piston that you hit with your hand or a mallet to a steel lever bench tool. As long as the corks have been well softened, they are all effective. Only new corks should ever be used. The quality varies. Use the best quality for wines to be stored for a number of years, making sure that the smoothest end is in contact with the wine. Corks of lesser quality may be used in bottles of wine that will be kept for months rather than years.

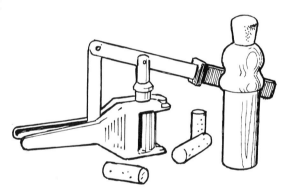

Coloured **foil** or **plastic capsules** protect the cork and impart a professional finish to the bottles. Very attractive **labels and collars** are available to designate the name and vintage of the wine. Most are plain backed and must be stuck on with gum. Ensure that no residue is left on the bottle at the edge of the label since this detracts from the appearance.

A **bottle rack** of some kind is needed in which to store the finished bottles on their side. There are many different kinds from which to choose, depending on the amount and shape of space that you have for this

13

Equipment for winemaking

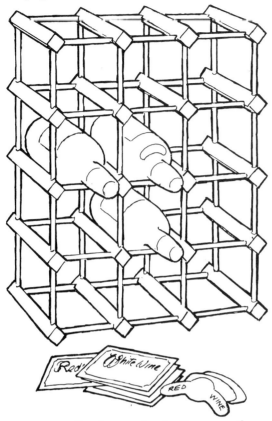

purpose. Racks can be built up to fit any shape, a sloping staircase for example. But they can become expensive and as a start you could use a few bottle cartons stored on their side.

Back into the realms of winemaking some other equipment is highly desirable. A long kitchen **thermometer** in a plastic case enables you to check the temperature of a must before the addition of a yeast, the temperature of water in which a dried yeast is to be regenerated, and the temperature of a sample of must or wine about to be tested with a hydrometer in a trial jar.

Every serious winemaker must have a **hydrometer** and a **trial jar**. The jar is just a tall cylindrical container to hold the sample to be tested. The hydrometer is a thermometer-shaped instrument, weighted at the bottom end and used to ascertain the specific gravity of the sample. It floats in the sample and a graduated chart contained in the upper

portion indicates the answer. In rather simplified terms this means the weight of the sugar present. With this piece of information we can easily calculate how much more sugar is needed to produce a wine of a required alcohol content. We can also follow the progress of a fermentation by noting the fall of the readings from say 1.090 to 0.990. There are many more uses for a hydrometer that will be described elsewhere; sufficient here to describe the instrument and emphasise its importance.

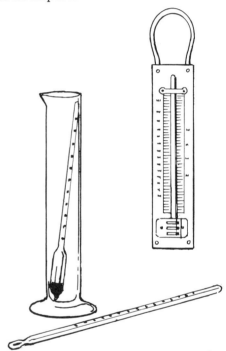

A means of checking the acidity of a must as well as its sweetness is also needed. Some winemakers use an **acid testing kit** and titrate a sample. Detailed instructions come with the inexpensive kit that consists of a conical flask, a test tube and small bottles of alkali and acid indicator. Other winemakers use **pH indicator papers** or simply an **acid testing paper** that when dipped in the sample to be tested merely indicates whether the acidity is low, normal or high. For most purposes the latter, albeit a rough guide, is adequate. There is no precise figure for any wine since many other variables affect the taste. It is important not to be too low nor too high and to this extent all musts should be checked in one way or another.

Some ingredients require mechanical help in their preparation. **Fruit crushers** are available for use on large quantities but few home winemakers can justify one. A stainless steel blade and shaft that can be attached to an electric drill is a tremendous help when crushing apples, and is not very expensive. **Liquidisers** are widely used for soft fruits and sultanas. A double boiler, called a **Saftborn**, is used by some winemakers for extracting juice. A small tap is fitted in the fruit container for running off the juice.

Nylon **straining bags** are available in different sizes and meshes, fine and large. Similarly with **sieves**. A selection is well worth having and often comes in useful when least expected.

A small **press** is needed for even moderate quantities of the larger fruits, notably apples. Whilst the cost may seem expensive at first, once bought it lasts for ever and saves an enormous amount of effort. At first, home winemakers make only one gallon at a time, but later they find that it is little more trouble to make five or ten gallons and this is when a press is most worthwhile.

There are now some 25-litre (5½-gallon) food grade plastic **fermentation bins** available for these larger quantities of must. Plastic cube-shaped containers in cardboard cartons make useful fermentation bins and temporary storage vessels for five-gallon quantities. They are used commercially for the sale of sherry by the glass and can sometimes be acquired from restaurants and hotels. Sterilise them before use.

Wooden casks have specific but limited value to the home winemaker. The minimum size safe to use is 25 litres (5½ gallons), and that for a period of around six months for red wines only. White wines are best matured in glass or stainless steel containers since an oaky flavour is not an advantage to them. Red wines *do* benefit from a period of maturation in oak, but the length of time depends on the size of the cask. The larger the cask the longer the wine may be left in it. But large casks are not easy to handle in the home; they must be supported on a cradle

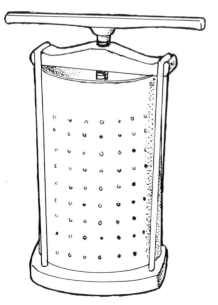

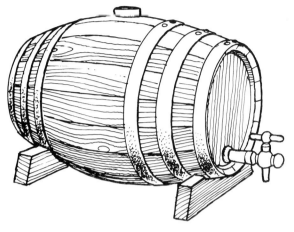

and kept in a cool and dry atmosphere. Each week they must be inspected and topped up with wine of the same or a similar kind so that no airspace develops and causes an over-oxidised flavour in the wine. A 25-litre cask is well worth having if you make at least two 5 gallon batches of red wine each year. Buy a new cask for preference or at least one that has been used for sherry or brandy or the like. *Do not* attempt to use one that has been used for vinegar; and one that has been used for beer is also questionable. A secondhand cask should be filled and also soaked in a bath of sulphited water for a day or two, so that the staves can swell and become tight and moisture-proof. After that it should be washed out with a hot and strong washing-soda solution. Pour two gallons of boiling water and a large handful of soda into the cask, fit the bung and roll the cask slowly up and down for at least 15 minutes, making sure that every part of the inside is frequently wetted. After draining, the cask must be rinsed with plenty of cold water and then filled with a sulphite solution, containing eight crushed Campden tablets and one level teaspoonful of citric acid per gallon. Leave this for two days, then empty and drain the cask. Next empty into it one bottle of a sound dry wine and swirl this round and round in the same way as the soda solution until the

cask is thoroughly seasoned. Drain out the wine, put the cask into a position where it can be easily filled and equally easily emptied, then fill it to the bung and bung tight.

Another use for a cask, especially an ex-sherry cask if you can get one, is for the storing of sherry-style wines. After the treatment just described, pour four gallons of sherry-style wine into the cask and as you draw off some wine, replace the quantity drawn off with another sherry-style wine, thus creating your own miniature solera. For this purpose the cask should not be filled to the bung.

Filtration is not often necessary, but a wine that will not clear naturally or with the assistance of finings should be filtered to produce the necessary brilliance required for exhibition purposes. **Filter kits** use either cellulose pads or powders. Full details on how to use the filter come with each kit and vary according to the filtration method used.

An even temperature is best for a good fermentation. To this end some winemakers need to encircle their jars with a **thermal belt** or stand them on a **thermal pad**. An **immersion heater** can also be bought to keep musts warm in cold situations. These appliances can all be connected to **thermostats** so that the correct heat is maintained. Alternatively, an insulated cupboard warmed by a low-wattage, black-bar heater may be used.

Finally, a **record book** should be used in which you can keep details of each wine made, ingredients, quantities, specific gravity before fermentation starts and after it finishes, the method used and an appraisal of the finished wine. The information from a record book is most helpful should a problem occur, and also if you wish to repeat a particular wine. It is also a useful *aide-mémoire* when discussing your wines with another person. **Record cards** attached to the vessels through fermentation and storage, and then kept in a loose-leaf binder are particularly useful.

3 Hygiene

The importance of cleanliness in making wine can hardly be over-emphasised. Long before the presence of micro-organisms was understood, those who made wine, mead, beer or cider used to scald their containers, burn sulphur in their casks and keep their brews covered. We now know that the air is full of moulds, fungi, bacteria and spores carried on the breeze or the movements of air due to rising or falling temperatures, both without and within the house. Wherever air can get, spoilage organisms can get, too; cupboards and drawers are no exception. When the air is still, the organisms settle on some surface and if they find food and moisture they begin to multiply at an alarming rate.

Sulphur is the longest known antidote and although there are now many more, sulphur remains one of the most effective and the safest, too. Sulphur matches are not much used today except by those with large casks or heavy or immovable containers or equipment. Most home winemakers now use sulphur in the form of sodium metabisulphite, a white powder commonly called sulphite. When dissolved in a liquid it releases a gas called sulphur dioxide which has a choking effect if it is inhaled. This gas can kill many weak organisms and inhibit the activity of the strong, including yeast.

Sulphite is sold loose in 100g (3½ oz) packets and upwards, as well as in a tablet form known as Campden tablets. These are hard and must first be crushed in the bowl of a spoon by the back of another. One tablet in solution releases 50 parts per million (ppm) of gas. Although more expensive, most winemakers use the tablets rather than the loose powder because of the known quantity in them. The effect of sulphur can be increased by the addition of citric acid.

A very strong sulphite solution can be made by dissolving eight crushed Campden tablets and one teaspoonful of citric acid in one pint of cold water. This solution is particularly effective for sterilising clean wine bottles, demijohns, trials jars, funnels, corks, bungs, straining bags, etc. Pour the solution into a jar, cover the mouth of the jar with your hand and shake the jar all ways to ensure that every piece of the surface is covered time and time again. The solution may now be poured through a funnel into another jar leaving the sterilised jar to drain. It is ready to receive wine without further rinsing.

The same solution can be used throughout a session of several hours, pouring it from one vessel to another, soaking bungs, corks or straining bags in it, filling siphons with it, washing larger equipment, such as polythene bins or a press, in fact every surface that can come into contact with wine, mead, beer or cider. Because of the presence of the citric acid the solution will not keep, but because it is so cheap it is worth making a fresh solution for every session.

Before sterilising the equipment, it should, of course, be clean and free from dirt. Dirty marks should be removed with a brush and the equipment should look clean to the eye. It may have to be washed in hot water containing a detergent, in which case the latter should be washed off with cold water before the piece of equipment is sterilised. Heavily stained equipment can be cleaned with a bleach solution or with a substance called Chempro which is also chlorine based. Great care must be taken to wash off the chlorine before use with plenty of cold water rinses. It will otherwise taint the beverage.

After demijohns have been in use for several years they become hazily discoloured. They should be left overnight full of cold water and Chempro or a bleach. Bungs and siphons, too, sometimes need a spring clean. Keeping all equipment clean, and sterilising it before use goes a long way towards producing sound wine.

The room in which the wine or other beverage is made should also be kept clean. Spilt must or wine should be wiped up at once and the floor washed in a sulphite or Chempro solution. It is sensible not to let colonies of spoilage organisms develop anywhere.

Immediately after use, all the equipment used should be washed clean, dried and put away. Before it is used again it should be rinsed and sterilised anew. Even newly bought equipment should be sterilised before use. Whilst this may all seem something of a nuisance, it quickly becomes part of the routine and does not seem a burden. Experience in both commercial wine and cidermaking and in every aspect of home brew indicates that proper attention to hygiene is time and effort well spent.

Ingredients, too, should be washed and whenever necessary, sterilised. All fruit should be cleaned free from stalks, leaves, grass, and damaged parts then rinsed in sulphite solution made from one gallon of cold water containing two crushed Campden tablets and a good pinch of citric acid crystals. By removing, killing or inhibiting

the spoilage organisms you provide a clean must in which the yeast can ferment. Again off-flavours are prevented. Vegetables that have to be boiled should be scrubbed clean from every trace of dirt before boiling them. Flowers and herbs must not be excluded from a sulphite solution for they are by their nature very attractive to spoilage organisms. In making wine, mead and cider at home you can't be too careful.

No must should left uncovered at any time, nor should it be unprotected. When a pectic enzyme is added to a must and left covered in a warm place for 24 hours, it should be protected by sulphite at the rate of one crushed Campden tablet per gallon.

Sulphite and citric acid is also an excellent anti-oxidant. When apples or pears are being crushed, or cut up, they should be dropped at once into a sulphite solution containing one crushed Campden tablet and a good pinch of citric acid for every gallon of wine being made. In this way the flesh of the apple will stay fresh and white and no hint of brown apple will affect the wine.

Before fruit is frozen it should be cleaned and washed in a sulphite solution, then drained and packed into cartons. Oxidation is prevented by thawing such fruit, if intended for winemaking, in a sulphite solution.

But sulphite must not be overdone. Too much sulphur can be tasted in a wine. Approximately half of it combines with minerals in the wine and becomes fixed. The right quantity is beneficial; too much is harmful. Remember, too, that sulphite can kill or at least inhibit yeast. Never add a yeast to a solution containing sulphite until 24 hours have elapsed, even then stir it well so that any remaining free gas can escape into the atmosphere.

Sulphite is your best friend if you use it wisely.

4 Wine kits

In a book on wines from the countryside, wine kits are of minor importance. The emphasis throughout this book is on wines and other drinks that you can make from indigenous rather than imported ingredients. Nevertheless, kits are of value, especially to beginners by helping them to obtain some practical experience quickly.

There are four qualities of wine kits: the Superior, the Standard, the Budget and the Express. The first three are usually packed to make six standard bottles of wine. The last one is often packed to make thirty bottles. A wide range of different styles of wine can be made: red, white, rosé, dry, sweet, vermouth-style, sherry-style, port-style, etc.

The Superior kits contain concentrated grape juice from good wine-growing areas and require no additional sugar in their making. The result can be a very satisfactory wine costing about one-fifth of its commercial counterpart. Standard kits also contain concentrated grape juice but some extra sugar is always required. Budget kits, as one would expect, cost less than the other two but sometimes contain fruit other than grape as well as flavourings and some single sugars. Additional household sugar is also required. Express kits contain not only concentrated fruit juice and flavourings but also a number of chemicals to assist in a very rapid fermentation and clearing of the wine. The

19

result is a light, quaffable wine rather than one to be sipped and savoured. Each kit contains detailed instructions on how to make it up and these should be followed very carefully. The instructions vary slightly from one manufacturer to another and have been worked out as the most suitable for the ingredients in the container.

If you have never made wine before, you are strongly recommended to make up one or two kits so that you get experience in the simple but essential activity of sterilising vessels, mixing the must, starting the yeast, fitting an airlock, watching the fermentation, racking the young wine, bottling, corking and, before long, tasting the result of your efforts.

Wines from country ingredients can be superior to wines from kits, but they do take longer to mature. It is good to have some wine to tide you over while your first country wine is still in the process.

Another use for concentrated grape juice, especially from standard kits, is in adding it to must from countryside ingredients. The grape contains sugar, tartaric acid, many minerals, vitamins and trace elements, all beneficial to fermentation and to the development of a good bouquet and vinous flavour. A small quantity added to the must improves the wine significantly. Sultanas or raisins, bottled grape juice or even fresh grapes may be added instead, but the concentrated grape juice is more convenient.

5 Fruit wines

PREPARING THE MUST

Must is the name given to a mixture of fruits, sugar and water (or vegetable liquor, etc.) prior to fermentation, after which it becomes wine. The preparation of the must really starts when gathering the fruit. Shrivelled, dried, damaged and poor quality ingredients cannot be expected to make the best wine. Whatever ingredient you are collecting do look for the very best available. Whilst plastic bags have great merits in certain matters, they are less satisfactory than baskets, cardboard cartons or strong paper carrier bags where fresh fruits are concerned. The plastic causes condensation of the humidity in the bag and makes the ingredients damp and prone to infection from omnipresent spoilage organisms.

Freezing

Fruits should always be used as soon as possible after their gathering, while they are still really fresh and before any deterioration has had time to begin. If it is not possible to start making wine with them at once, then clean and freeze them until it is convenient. Cleaning involves the removal of stalks, washing them in a weak sulphite solution (50 ppm), and removing any stones (e.g. from peaches or plums). The fruit should then be packed into vapour proof boxes with close-fitting lids or thick plastic bags secured very tightly at the neck with a wire tie. In this packaging they will keep in good condition for many months. Very large fruit, e.g. apples and pears, should be cut into eighths,

dropped in a citric acid and sulphite solution (100 ppm), and left for several minutes, drained and then packed. Fruits should, as far as possible, be frozen in the condition in which they are to go into the must. It is not easy to work on ingredients that have been frozen without proper cleaning. Elderberries, for example, that are simply frozen as picked are extremely difficult to separate from their stems. Tiny portions of stem break off with the berry and cause excess bitterness in the wine.

After freezing, the fruit can be thawed in a few minutes in a microwave oven, or in a few hours in a refrigerator, but perhaps the best way is to thaw them in a weak sulphite solution (50 ppm) so that oxidation is prevented.

Pectin reduction

As soon as the fruit is ready, it should be crushed or liquidised. All white fruits should be placed in a sterilised bin containing cold water, pectic enzyme, one crushed Campden tablet per gallon of wine being made, together with any acid required by the recipe. Cover the bin and leave it in a warm place (24°C/75°F) for 24 hours. Almost all fruits contain pectin – the setting factor in jam-making – and this needs to be broken down for winemaking. The pectin-reducing enzyme is marketed under such names as Pectinase, Pectolin, Pectozyme or Pectolytic enzyme and directions regarding the quantity to be used are given on the packet. Keep the packets of powder or tablets in a cool, dry place and the bottle of liquid enzyme in a cool, dark place. The liquid enzyme has a shorter shelf life than the powder or tablets.

It is very important to include the crushed Campden tablet at this stage for this protects the crushed fruit from infection and oxidation while the enzyme is at work on the pectin. Even so, the bin should be closely covered to prevent access by unwanted visitors. Enzymes that break down pectin prefer to operate in a comfortably warm situation and are more effective in a fairly low sugar solution.

Based on research in the commercial wine industries, some amateur winemakers add bentonite to their musts at this stage so that when the pulp is strained and pressed it is cleaner than it would otherwise be. It should not be added too soon, however, and the day after fermentation begins is adequate for normal purposes since our quantities are so much smaller. Furthermore, the presence of bentonite inhibits the break down of the pectin.

Black fruits contain colour in their skins and this is best extracted by pouring hot water over the crushed fruit and leaving it to cool in a covered bin. The pectin enzyme is then added and the must is again left covered, in the same way as white fruits, for 24 hours.

Acidity

After the fruit has been soaked in the liquor for 24 hours, the must should be tested for acidity by titration, by pH measurement, or at least by an acid-indicator paper. Of the three main fruit acids, *tartaric* is found only in grapes; *malic* is found in grapes and in many other fruits, notably apples from which its name is derived; and *citric* is found in small quantities in grapes and also in a number of other fruits, notably the citrus fruits from which its name is derived.

Citric is the least expensive of the three and is the most widely used, but it is worth considering the nature of the main acid in the ingredient and adding one of the other two. If some grape is to be included in the must then choose one of the two acids not in the other fruit.

Citric acid ensures a good fermentation, but some judges of wine are of the opinion that it imparts a hard finish to a wine – a view not generally shared, however. Malic acid imparts a fruity taste to the wine, but is subject to partial reduction to lactic acid when fermentation is finished, and sometimes not until after the wine has been bottled. Carbon dioxide is released during the reduction and is often the cause of a blown cork. Tartaric acid is thought to convey the most wine-like flavour of the three but it is insoluble in the presence of alcohol at very low temperatures. As a result, tiny glass-like crystals may form on the base of the cork, on the side of a bottle or in the punt (the indentation of the bottom of the bottle) during storage in a cold place. The wine loses a little of its appealing appearance in bottle but is none the worse and usually smoother to taste than it would otherwise be.

Table wines need from 5 to 7 parts acid per thousand parts (ppt) wine. Sweet and dessert wines need from 6 to 9 parts depending on the sweetness, body and alcohol content. One level 5ml spoonful of acid is roughly equal to one part per thousand in a gallon of wine.

Acid is an essential part of the bouquet and flavour of a wine and a wine that is low in acid tastes dull and insipid. The yeast cells also need an acid solution in which to flourish and they form a number of new acids, notably succinic acid which contributes to the winey smell. The quantity of acid formed during fermentation varies from 1 to 2 parts per thousand (ppt). A must starting at 4 ppt may be increased to 6 ppt, while one beginning at 7 ppt may only increase to 8 ppt. Acid is also essential to the keeping quality of a wine. During maturation some of the acids combine with the different alcohols to form aldehydes and sweet-smelling esters, thus diminishing the total acidity. There is no precise figure for any wine and only general guidelines can be given and followed.

Fruits, of course, contain varying quantities of acid depending on their nature, variety, ripeness, the soil in which they were grown and the sun and rain they received during their growing. Some fruits, like blackcurrants, have an abundant supply of acid, others like pears, are deficient. It is important, then, to check the acidity and to adjust it as necessary by the incorporation of an appropriate acid in the necessary quantity for the style of wine being made.

Sugar

After checking the acidity, the must should be tested for its natural sugar content. For this we use a hydrometer and trial jar. After giving the must a good stir, a jugful of fruit liquor should be removed and strained through a nylon sieve into a funnel inserted into the trial jar. Fill the jar almost to the top but leave room for the hydrometer. As far as possible exclude particles of pulp. Insert the hydrometer slowly and carefully so that it does not bounce on the bottom or swing wildly. As soon as it is still and floating freely, read the figure on the line at the bottom of the saucer-shaped meniscus. This is the natural gravity of the must and by reference to the hydrometer tables on page 114 you can see the weight of sugar that the reading represents. The vast majority of the specific gravity of a must is due to sugar, but there is likely to be some acid present and may be other items that could marginally distort the true sugar content. If you wish to keep some very accurate records, you could deduct four points from the last figure of your reading, although few people do so. There are so many variables that precise accounting is not likely to affect the finished wine sufficiently for it to be noticeable. But, as with the rough tests for acid, it is important to have some idea of the sugar content.

Knowing the kind of wine that you are making means that you also have an idea as to its appropriate alcohol content.

A light white wine should contain around 10% alcohol
A full-bodied, dry white table wine between 11 and 12%
A sweet white table wine around 12%
A rosé wine between 10.5 and 11.5%
A dry red table wine from 11.5 to 13.5%
A social wine around 13%
An aperitif from 14 to 16%
An after-dinner dessert wine from 14 to 17%, unless fortified with spirit
A sparkling wine around 11% prior to the secondary fermentation.

By noting the sugar content figure adjacent to the specific gravity reading on the same line as the chosen alcohol content, and by deducting the sugar content figure on the same line as the specific gravity reading of your sample of must, you can calculate the quantity of sugar that you must add to achieve a wine of the required alcohol content. Again, because of the many variables, this alcohol content is approximate, rather than precise; nevertheless, it is a very good guide and is not likely to be out by more than $1°$ of alcohol at the most.

With the acid level checked and adjusted and the sugar level checked and noted, the yeast may now be incorporated into the must and fermentation started.

Fermentation

Only a few day's pulp fermentation is necessary, taking care to keep the pulp submerged or gently pressed down into the liquor twice each day. This pressing down should be gentle enough so as not to incorporate too much air into the must, but sufficient to keep the pulp wet. Keep the vessel well covered, but not so closely as to prevent the fermentation gas from escaping. The atmospheric temperature surrounding the bin should be between 13°C (55°F) and 17°C (62°F) for white and rosé wines, and from 18°C (64°F) to 21°C (70°F) for red wines.

After the appropriate period of pulp fermentation, strain out the solids through a nylon straining bag and press them dry. Mix up the pulp in the bag from time to time until all the juice has been extracted when the pulp may be discarded. Stir the appropriate quantity of sugar into the must, pour it into a demijohn, fit an airlock and continue the fermentation.

YEAST AND THE MIRACLE OF FERMENTATION

Leaven of bread had been known for thousands of years and ale yeast, too, but it wasn't until 1837, when the first microscopes became available, that it was discovered that beer and wine yeasts were spherical and single-cell members of the plant world, needing nitrogen to live and thrive. Chemists of the early nineteenth century, however, would not accept that these cells caused the conversion of sugar to alcohol. They earnestly believed that fermentation was spontaneous or was caused by oxygen.

Napoleon III, in 1863, concerned about the quantity of wine that soured on its way to the consumer, invited Louis Pasteur to investigate the problem. After a series of experiments he was able to prove that yeast cells did cause fermentation. He also proved that wine exposed to air allowed the growth of vinegar bacteria, as well as causing the colour to fade from either red or white to tawny shades. He wrote his first masterpiece *Études sur le vin*, which was followed by one on beer.

Later, scientists discovered that the yeast cell contains a number of enzymes that convert the sugar one step at a time through more than 15 different stages to alcohol and carbon dioxide. Further research has shown that there are around 1,000 different varieties of yeast, only a few of which are beneficial in the making of alcoholic beverages. Of these the most important is *saccharomyces cerevisiae*. This yeast has a number of sub-varieties, one of which is the wine yeast *saccharomyces cerevisiae elipsoideus*. This, too, has a number of different strains that produce marginally different results. These

are generally called by the name of the grape wine to which they appear to be indigenous. We know them as Hock, Port, Sherry, Champagne, Burgundy, etc. When used with a sympathetic must they add significance and distinction to the finished wine. The recipes take account of this and different strains are recommended. There is, however, an all-purpose strain which may be used if you so prefer. It is important for the best results, however, always to use a wine yeast when making wine, mead and cider. The granulated yeast sold for making bread or beer is not suitable for making wine. That used for bread ferments very quickly, almost explosively – it has to for bread. This violent fermentation causes a dissipation of some of the ethers being formed as well as an overflow of the wine. Furthermore, bread yeast fails to impart a good flavour and is frequently unwilling to settle firmly, making racking very difficult.

The yeast for making beer also ferments rapidly and on the surface at that, forming great clouds of foam. It can impart a hoppy or beery taste to wine if used for that purpose.

Worst of all, however, is failure to use a yeast at all, relying on the wild yeast that grows on the skin of fruits. These wild yeasts are often mixed up with bacteria and other spoilage organisms. Moreover, they can rarely produce more than four per cent alcohol.

It is a waste of your time and trouble, then, not to use a proper wine yeast. One sachet of yeast will produce more than 30 bottles of wine. Spread over such a number the cost is minimal when you remember all the savings on duty, tax, transport, overheads and profit, even on the cheapest wine.

Wine yeast is available as a dried yeast, both in loose granules and pressed tablet form. It can also be bought on slivers of dried rose hip shells or floating in distilled water contained in a sealed phial. A pure culture form can sometimes be bought on an agar slant in a test tube, sealed in a laboratory.

When bought, yeast should be stored in a

cool, dark place until required. The door of a refrigerator is ideal. Packets and sachets should be kept sealed, for the dried yeast deteriorates if exposed to the air. It is best to buy yeast as you need it, or no more than your likely requirements over the next two or three months. Drums or containers of yeast from which you take a spoonful at a time are not recommended.

Before use, the yeast should be re-activated in tepid water 40–45°C (104 –113°F). The dormant cells absorb the moisture in a matter of minutes and are then ready for mixing into a must. It helps if the tepid water contains a little strained orange juice and sugar, or better still, a little grape juice. Some yeasts are packed in sealed sachets containing a little sugar and nutrient salt and need nothing but the tepid water.

When yeast is reproducing itself it needs oxygen, so stir the yeast starter to mix in some air. Similarly, when the starter is added to the must, stir it well before covering it with a lid or fitting an airlock. Once a large colony has been developed, yeast can live without air, and it is at this stage that most of the alcohol is formed. This is the reason for fitting an airlock to a fermenting must. It keeps out the air!

The yeast cannot thrive without nitrogen, however. Many fruits and vegetables contain nitrogenous matter, but it is always best to be on the safe side and include 2.5 ml (½ level tsp) ammonium phosphate or sulphate, or a mixture of both, usually called yeast nutrient with the yeast. Insufficient nitrogen in a must encourages the production of fusel oils one of which, amyl alcohol, combines with acetic acid to form amyl acetate, the unpleasant 'pear drop' smell. Vitamin B_1 is also needed by yeast and some winemakers always include one 3 mg Benerva tablet. Only a tiny quantity is required and some fruits contain enough, and to spare – notably the grape. It makes very good sense, then, to include some grape in every must. In addition to the measure of sugar it contains, the grape also contributes tartaric acid and traces

of many vitamins and mineral salts beneficial to the yeast, thus ensuring a trouble-free fermentation. Without vitamin B_1 hydrogen sulphide, the bad-egg smell, may be formed.

Yeast also needs an acid solution in which to thrive. Even very old recipes included the juice of a lemon. Citric acid is still the most commonly used acid, but in crystal form rather than as lemon juice. Where the nature of the acid in a fruit is known, however, for example in the apple which contains malic acid, it is sensible to include one or both of the other two acids – citric or tartaric, the acid found only in the grape.

Finally, yeast likes an even, warm temperature in which to be active. It will function in the range of 5° to 35°C (41° to 95°F), but these are extremes and it functions poorly at both ends. It prefers the range 20° to 24°C (68°–75°F), free from fluctuations. Experience shows us, however, that white wines develop better bouquet and flavour when they are fermented in the range of 13° to 17°C (55° to 62°F). Red wines on the other hand benefit from a slightly higher fermentation temperature, 18° to 21°C (64° to 70°F). Fermentation generates a few degrees of heat and the temperature of the must is likely to be slightly in excess of the atmospheric temperature.

Thermal belts to fit around demijohns, and thermal pads on which to stand jars, are available from specialist shops. They are sometimes fitted with a thermostat. To ensure a successful fermentation as far as their product is concerned, manufacturers often set them too high, usually at 24°C (75°F) and because the thermostat is an inexpensive one, it is likely to need a fluctuation of 5°C (9°F) before it switches on or off. However, these are not adjustable.

Soon after a yeast is added to a must it sometimes happens that there is a tumultuous ferment and the must boils over. The word ferment comes from the French *fervere*, meaning 'to boil'. This is usually caused by the presence of too much fruit or vegetable pulp in the must and the jar being too full. It is better not to fill the jar right to the neck at first, so as to leave some headroom for the foaming. When it is finished, after two or three days, top up the jar with water. Better still, save some of the sugar, say 340g (12 oz), dissolve this in sufficient water and add this to the jar. Another way is to remove half a bottle or so of must and to ferment this beside the jar at first, mixing it in later.

A table wine should ferment right out to dryness within two to three weeks. Curiously, some ferment out in five or six days whilst others take as many weeks. It is impossible to be more precise in guidance on this point because of the many variable factors involved.

Occasionally a fermentation will stop prematurely and cause you to wonder why. The very first check must be with a hydrometer. Siphon a portion of the must into a sterilised trial jar and insert a hydrometer. It may well be that, to your astonishment, all the sugar has been converted and fermentation is finished. Should this not be so, however, then you must seek some other reason.

Causes and remedies for a stuck fermentation are as follows.

1 The must has become too hot or too cold – check the temperature of the must – and if needs be move it to a cooler or a warmer place. This problem can occur during extremes of weather conditions. During a heatwave it might be possible to stand the jar in a bucket of cold water and to cover it with cloths soaked in water. In bitter weather, stand the jar close to a fire or boiler until fermentation starts and then wrap the jar in a blanket or in sheets of newspaper.

2 You may have, inadvertently, omitted the acid or nutrients when preparing the must. Check your record card and if true, make amends. But it is not always easy to re-start a must in these circumstances. Additionally, give the wine an airing by pouring it into a bin and give it a good stir, then return it to the jar and stand it in a warm place, 24°C (75°F), for a few days.

3 Sometimes a must can become choked with carbon dioxide and the airing just described releases the molecules of gas into quite a foam.

4 It may be that too much sugar was added at first and that the yeast has fermented to the limit of its tolerance. Or worse, that the weight of sugar has killed the yeast. If the density of the must is greater than that of the fluids in the yeast cell, the cell walls will collapse. For this reason, it is sensible to start the fermentation with only a moderate quantity of sugar, say with a specific gravity no higher than 1.090 and preferably lower. More sugar can be mixed in during fermentation to form high-alcohol aperitif and dessert wines.

5 Fermentation often stops if a must is racked from its sediment before fermentation has finished. Although a heavy deposit may be apparent, it is best not to remove it until fermentation is complete. If premature racking is the cause you may have to add another yeast.

If all the remedies suggested fail and you have to add a fresh yeast, a certain procedure should be followed. When the new yeast has been regenerated in tepid water and is seen to be vigorously active, add to it a similar volume of stuck must, measure for measure. For example, if you have a quarter pint of activated yeast, add to it a quarter pint of stuck must. If you have half a pint then add half a pint. When this is working well, add another equal measure, i.e. a pint to a pint. When that is working well add another equal measure, i.e. a quart to a quart. Continue until all the must has been added and is working. Adding a fresh yeast direct to a stuck must rarely starts fermentation. Adding a stuck must in equal measures to a fermenting starter usually succeeds.

Terminating fermentation
It sometimes happens that you wish to make a sweet wine of relatively low alcohol, say 11 or 12%, as opposed to one of 14 or 15%. Fermentation can be checked by racking the must from its sediment into a demijohn containing one gramme of potassium sorbate and one crushed Campden tablet. Seal the jar and store it in a cold place for a week or so while the wine clears, then siphon out the wine through a filter. The clear wine will be both sweet and stable. Potassium sorbate is usually marketed in a drum with a lid that is recommended by the manufacturer for use in measuring the quantity required. It is also available in tablet form. A trade name such as 'sorbistat' may be used to describe either the powder or the tablet.

Fermentation on the pulp
Many fruit wines begin with a period of fermentation of the crushed fruit and water. This is the traditional way of extracting colour, flavour, sugar, acid, etc. from the ingredients. Only a few days of such fermentation are required, varying from three to six, depending on the fruit. Before the yeast is added, a portion of the must should be removed and pressed and the liquid poured into a trial jar. Insert a hydrometer and note on your records the specific gravity of the must. This will give you an approximation of the sugar content. There will be some fruit extract, acids, tannins and other substances present as well as sugar, and an allowance of up to four points should be allowed for them. You can now calculate how much extra sugar to add at a later date to achieve the alcohol content you desire, by referring to the hydrometer tables on page 114. First, look at the potential alcohol column and select the figure appropriate to the wine being made. Now note the quantity of sugar per gallon on the same line as your alcohol figure. From this deduct the quantity of sugar per gallon on the line indicated by the hydrometer reading of your must. The difference is the additional sugar required.

After the yeast has been added, stir the must thoroughly and cover the vessel with a loosely fitting lid or a thick cloth to keep out the spoilage micro-organisms floating in the air. The pulp will be raised above the surface of the liquid content by the bubbles of the carbon dioxide. It must be kept submerged by a china plate weighted, if necessary, by a bottle containing sufficient water for the purpose. Both plate and bottle should be sterilised, of course, in a sulphite solution.

Alternatively, the floating fruit cap must be pressed down twice a day and gently mixed into the liquid. Failure to do this will result in an inadequate extraction from the fruit and the raised pulp will become infected with spoilage bacteria – notably the vinegar bug!

During pulp fermentation some alcohol is formed but not much. After the fruit has been strained out and pressed dry, the appropriate quantity of sugar calculated as described above should be mixed in and completely dissolved. The now all-liquid must should be poured into a demijohn and fermentation continued under an airlock.

As a result of the many chemical changes that take place during fermentation a number of new acids are formed, notably proprionic, valerianic, glutannic and succinic, the latter being largely responsible for the winey smell. This increases the acidity of the wine by up to two parts per thousand. Sometimes afterwards, however, especially in red wines, some malic acid may be converted into lactic acid and carbon dioxide. This may produce only a slight prickle of bubbles or may be enough to blow out a cork. In white wines containing tartaric acid that have been stored in a very cold place, some of the tartaric acid may be precipitated as potassium tartrate crystals making the wine smoother to the palate.

All these various developments and changes are part of the miracle of fermentation. In 1814, this was described in a book by a Mr Cushing. He wrote: 'Vinous fermentation may be said to be a divine operation which the omniscient Creator has placed in our cup of life, to transmute the fruits of the earth into wine for the benefit and comfort of His creatures!' A nice thought that isn't spoiled by now knowing how it happens.

FINAL STAGES

There is an opinion among some winemakers that, having carefully selected and balanced the ingredients, the wine should be left 'to make itself'. Indeed, the first piece of advice given to me when I was shown how to make wine in August 1945, was 'Don't worry the wine'. Experience shows that this is sensible advice, especially during the period of fermentation, but at the end it is essential to remove the young wine from its deposit of decomposing particles of pulp and dead yeast cells. This process is called racking. At one time there was a widespread belief that wine should only be racked 'while the moon was waning, the wind was from some northerly quarter and the day serene and free from thunder'! There seems to be no scientific evidence to support this theory, but there are very good reasons for racking as soon as fermentation is finished. Failure to do so enables the decomposing debris to impart a foul taste to the wine. Furthermore, the act of racking often helps a hazy wine to clear.

If the container in which you have been fermenting your wine has a tap, this can be opened so that the clear wine can flow into another container beneath. The sediment will have settled below the tap level. The more customary method, however, is to siphon the clearing wine into another container with the aid of a piece of plastic tubing.

A simple tap can be fitted into one end of the tube so that the flow can be regulated. A J-tube can be attached to the other end so that the clear wine is sucked down into the tube without disturbing the sediment. If the tube is passed through a bored bung fitted into the neck of the jar, it will hold the tube steady. It will be necessary to have a vent hole in the bung to admit air as the wine is drawn out. Alternatively, a bored bung can be cut into two along the length of the bore and the two pieces may then be used as wedges.

Place the jar of wine to be racked on a work surface and the sterilised receiving container on the floor beneath. Insert the J-tube end of the siphon into the jar of wine and suck on the other end of the tube. As soon as the tube is full, squeeze the end and place it in the empty jar, then the wine will flow until only the sediment remains. Should there be a quantity of cloudy wine and sediment left, pour this into a bottle and store this in a cold place until the sediment again settles, leaving clear wine above to be siphoned off.

The process of racking necessarily admits air to the wine. This can be minimised by causing the wine to flow quietly down the side of the receiving jar rather than splashing it in the middle. Better still, let the wine flow beneath the surface rather than on top of it. The admission of some air is beneficial to the development of the wine, but if too much is admitted the wine may oxidise and fade. It could also become infected from spoilage organisms in the air. As a safety measure, then, always add one Campden tablet per gallon of wine racked. In addition, and even more importantly, keep all jars and containers 'full to the bung'.

The removal of sediment usually reduces the quantity of wine by a margin and this must be made up in some way. The best method is to top up with a similar style wine. Top up a dry wine only with another dry wine. The addition of a small quantity of sweet wine may cause a secondary fermentation. But the wine does not have to be from

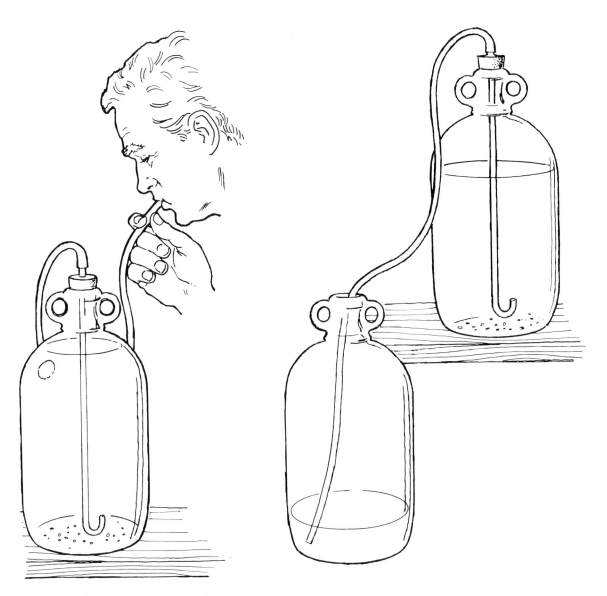

the same ingredient; a rhubarb may be used with a gooseberry, or the latter with an apple or any other combination. A little white could even be added to a red, but not the other way! The addition of another wine is more likely to benefit the new wine than change its character.

If no wine is available, a small quantity, up to half a pint per gallon, of cold boiled water may be used. The dilution is unlikely to be noticeable. Other alternatives include the insertion of sterilised glass marbles or beach pebbles.

The jar should now be sealed and labelled, and stored in a cool, dark place free from vibration. Each one must solve this problem in the light of their own facilities. Some winemakers have an underground cellar, others have a trap door in the floorboards through which they can reach the cavity beneath. Some use a brickbuilt garage or outhouse, others a spare bedroom, or a space under the stairs. The loft is an obvious store room, but care should be taken to ensure that it does not become too hot in summer. The precise temperature of the wine store is not critical, 10°C (50°F) is the ideal, but 15°C (59°F), or even 20°C (68°F), is acceptable provided the fluctuations are minimal.

In this connection, earthenware storage jars are ideal since their very thickness acts as an insulation, keeping the wine within well-protected from sudden changes in temperature. Plastic containers are not recommended for long storage. All too often the plastic is not vapourproof and the wine suffers deterioration. Glass or earthenware jars are undoubtedly best for small quantities. An oak cask, suitably clean and sterilised, may be used for a short period, especially for red wines and very strong wines. The smallest cask it is safe to use is the 25-litre (5½-gallon) size and this for no longer than six months at a time. The oak staves permit the admission of some air which is good for the wine up to a point. They also impart an oaky flavour to a wine, which is good in certain quantities. But both air and oak can spoil a wine after a while. Six months for red wine in a small cask is often beneficial, longer can cause deterioration. It all has to do with the ratio of the surface of the wine in contact with the oak to the total volume of wine in the cask. The larger the cask used the longer the

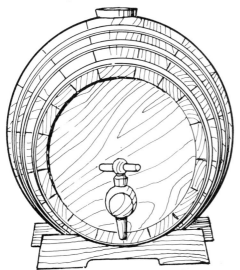

wine may be left in it. Even so, the cask must be examined at frequent intervals – every other week at least – and any ullage, or air space beneath the bung, filled with wine of a similar type. The cask must be kept full to the bung. The cask must also be stored on a cradle so that the weight is supported near the end planks. If the belly staves carried the weight they would open slightly and weep.

Most wines clear naturally if left in a cool place, preferably on a cold floor. The absence of thermal currents, i.e. warm wine rising from the bottom, usually allows solid particles, no matter how light and small, to settle down. Very occasionally, however, a wine will not clear to brilliance and some finings must be added. A number of manufacturers market proprietary brands of fining agents. Use them as directed but only when necessary. Fining often removes tannin from a wine as well as those solid particles not required.

Hazes usually consist of pectin, protein, cellulose, tissue and micro-organisms. Pectin can be removed by the addition of sufficient pectolytic enzyme, best added before fermentation begins. It is not responsive to the usual fining agents. Its presence can be detected by mixing one teaspoonful of wine with two tablespoonfuls of methylated spirits in a small bottle. Shake the mixture well and then leave it to stand for up to an hour. Hold the bottle up to a light and if the mixture contains solid dots or strings then the haze is caused by pectin.

Starch haze is rare in home-made wines unless cereals have been used. Its presence can be detected by the addition of a few drops of iodine to some wine in the centre of a white saucer. If the wine darkens or turns blue, starch is present. It can be removed with fungal amylase used in accordance with the manufacturer's instructions.

Should finings fail to clear a wine adequately it should be filtered in accordance with the instructions that come with the filter. A good case can be made for cleaning up a hazy wine as soon as possible after fermentation and leaving it to mature in a pristine state.

Wines mature unevenly. One year a wine from a particular recipe will be ready for drinking in six months. In another year, it may need twelve months or longer. Different wines, too, need different periods of maturation and the recommendations given in the recipes can be no more than a guide. From time to time a wine should be tasted, and experience will soon show you when it is ready for drinking. When bottling your wines, then, it makes good sense to use some half-size bottles as well as the standard size. Four half-size bottles and four standard per gallon are best at first, but two and five are better than all standard.

Use only proper wine bottles that have been washed inside and out and labels removed. Sterilise them with a sulphite solution, fill them to within 2 cm (¾ in) of the bottom of the cork and fit a cylindrical cork that has been soaked for several hours in a sulphite solution to soften and sterilise it.

There are a number of different corking tools available to help drive the cork home flush. A plastic or metal foil can be fitted over the cork and neck to give a neat finish. Attractive collars and labels can also be used to differentiate the wines. It is impossible to tell by sight alone, for example, whether a wine is made from apple, gooseberry or rhubarb. Every bottle should have a label of some sort giving its name and vintage. The bottles should be stored on their sides to keep the corks moist and swollen, thus ensuring a tight fit. If a wine rack is not available, bottle cartons laid on their sides may be used.

Some wines made in large quantities and served regularly with meals may be put into double-skinned plastic bags fitted with taps and supported in a carton. A number of commercial wines are now marketed in this way. Empty bags and cartons may be bought and used in the home. Much time is saved in bottling and the wine in the bag does not spoil when some is drawn off since the soft plastic collapses on to the wine and excludes air. After use the bag may be washed, sterilised and used many times over. Keep a boxed bag of white wine in the refrigerator and it is always ready for use. Store a boxed bag of red wine in the kitchen and that, too, is always available. Surprisingly to critics of home winemakers, these boxed bags of readily available wine do not lead to over-indulgence. On the contrary, since only one glass need be drawn off at a time. If a bottle is opened there is a tendency to finish it in case the portion remaining should spoil. In fact, most home-made wines will last for two or three days after opening and some may even improve.

Blending

However much care is taken in making the different wines some wines turn out less well than was hoped for. The number of variable factors makes it virtually impossible to make exactly similar wines from the same recipe. Inevitably, some will be better than others. This is equally true in the commercial world of wine and we should imitate their response to the situation. Far too many home wine-makers regard every wine they make as a swan, even though some are ducks! The 'ducks' can be turned into 'swans' by blending them together.

There are few guidelines and only one rule in blending. The rule is never to include a wine that smells and tastes bad. It may well have an infection that could spoil the other wines. Blend together, then, only sound wines that are lacking in flavour or that have too much flavour, or that are too sweet or too sharp. There is nothing to stop you blending white with red if you so wish. Mix the wines together in a bin, then siphon them back into clean jars. Fit airlocks for a week or two in case fermentation should start again. After about one month the wines are usually sufficiently homogenised to be ready for drinking and will always taste better than any of the individual wines that are in it.

This practice is especially important in the making of apple wine by those with access to a number of different varieties of apples that mature at different times in the season from August through to December. In the following Spring all the different batches of apple wines can be mixed together making one harmonious wine. Similarly with sherry-style wines. A blend of several such wines will always produce a better wine. Indeed, all commercial sherries are blends of wines from different years. Blending is an art that is well worth cultivating.

SPARKLING WINES

In the last century, champagne was often described as the King of Wines and the Wine of Kings. It was and still is *the* wine to drink on very special occasions. It might have been expected, then, that sparkling wines would now be widely made in the home. Alas, this is not so, although it is not very difficult to make excellent sparkling wine if you so wish.

It is important to intend to make a sparkling wine from the outset, rather than to attempt to sparkle an existing wine. Begin by selecting a suitable base ingredient such as apple, apricot, gooseberry, grapes, pear, rhubarb, whitecurrant. Use only sufficient ingredients to give you a delicate rather than a dominant flavour and make up the body with some white grapes, or grape juice, or concentrated grape juice or sultanas.

Carefully check and control the sugar content so that no more than 11% alcohol is produced – a little under doesn't matter, a little over does.

Use a champagne-wine yeast and add some nutrient and vitamin B_1 to ensure a complete fermentation to dryness in as even a temperature as you can maintain between 15°C and 18°C (low to middle 60°F).

As soon as fermentation is finished check the specific gravity of the wine. It should be in the range 0.992–0.996. If it is above this figure, i.e. 1.000 or higher, then give the wine a good stir up and stand the jar in a warmer place for a few days until the last of the sugar has been fully fermented.

If the wine is reasonably clear, pass it through a good filter. Some filters involve the use of fining ingredients including sulphite and may not require an added Campden tablet. Follow the filtering instructions on your equipment. Store the wine for six months in a cool place, 10–15°C (50–59°F), making sure that the jar is well sealed and labelled.

If the wine is still very hazy, store it in a really cold place – the refrigerator, perhaps – for a few days to encourage the solids to settle down, then filter it.

After maturing the wine for 6 months or more, activate another champagne yeast, add a pinch of nutrient and precisely 70g (2½ oz) sugar per gallon of wine. This quantity of sugar is quite critical to ensure an appropriate sparkle in a completely dry wine. If the wine is not completely dry the new yeast and additional sugar may create too much pressure. If more sugar is used than that recommended then the same result will be achieved – too much pressure. If insufficient sugar is used the result will be a wine with a poor sparkle. Make sure, then, that the wine is dry and that the correct amount of sugar is used. It must be completely dissolved and a little of the wine may be used for this purpose. One way is to remove half a cupful of wine from the jar, place this in a small saucepan and warm it to 40°C (104°F). Stir in the yeast and fifteen minutes later the sugar. As soon as the sugar is dissolved, pour the sweetened wine and activated yeast back into the jar of star-bright wine, free from any deposit or sediment. Fit an airlock and leave the jar in a warm place (24°C/75°F). Within a few hours fermentation should be seen to have started and the wine should now be bottled.

Use only proper heavy champagne bottles that are free from labels, scratches and chips, and sterilise them in the normal way. Fill each bottle only to within 5 cm (2 in) of the top for this air gap is essential. Next press home plastic hollow-domed stoppers that have been softened in hot water. Make sure that the fit is absolutely tight, then wire on a cage called a muselet.

Lay the bottles on their sides after giving each one a shake and listening to the stopper to ensure that no hissing sound can be heard, implying an imperfect seal. It is important in the making of a sparkling wine to conduct this secondary fermentation in the bottle and while the bottle is lying on its side. This position in a warm room facilitates the conversion of the additional sugar more effectively.

After five or six days the wine should be moved to a cool store whilst the champagne flavour is developed. A period of at least six months should be allowed for this and the bottles must continue to lie in the same position on their sides.

A feather-like sediment will be deposited on the lower side of the bottle and this has to be eased into the hollow dome of the stopper. A bottle carton set at an angle of 45° does well for this. Place the bottles in the carton, stopper first, and every few days give each bottle a gentle knock and twist to encourage

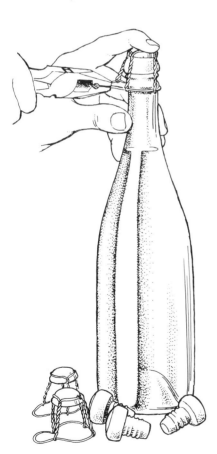

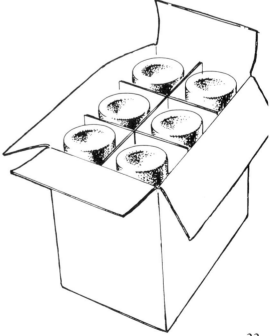

the sediment to slide down the side towards the stopper. Gradually, too, the carton can be stood upright until the bottles are vertically upside down. This process may take 3 or 4 weeks to complete, but it doesn't occupy many moments at any one time. As soon as the wine is bright and the sediment is in the stopper the wine is ready for the next process – disgorging the sediment.

If possible, stand the bottles, still upside down of course, in the refrigerator for several hours or overnight. Then take a trayful of ice cubes, place them in a plastic bag and crush them with a mallet or rolling pin. Put the crushed ice in a basin and mix into it one rounded tablespoonful of cooking salt. Take one bottle at a time and plunge the stopper and neck in the ice. It helps to do this in a cool corner where the bottle can be supported for about 10 minutes. Some refrigerators have shelves with flaps in them especially for tall bottles. It may be possible to put the bowl of crushed ice and salt on a lower shelf and pass the head of the bottle through the gap in the upper shelf. This would not only support the bottle, but also keep it cold.

After about 8–10 minutes the wine in the neck of the bottle will be seen to be frozen. The bottle can now be removed and another put in its place. Revert the bottle to the upright, undo the wire and remove the cage, ease out the stopper containing the sediment and frozen wine and promptly replace it with a clean stopper previously softened in hot water. But a totally dry sparkling wine is not very attractive to many people. Just before fitting the new stopper then, pop into the bottle one or, at the most, two saccharin pellets. One takes the edge off the dryness and leaves a pleasantly dry taste, two imparts a little sweetness to the wine.

The process of removing one stopper and pushing home the next takes only a matter of a second or so. If the right amount of sugar was used and the wine was well-chilled, there will be no foaming. Wire on the cage and the wine can be labelled and set aside for drinking when required. Repeat this process for each bottle. No further maturation is necessary. Serve the wine in tall, flute-shaped glasses at a temperature of about 8°C (46°F).

SHERRY-STYLE WINES

The golden rule when storing wines is to keep the containers full so as to exclude air and avoid over-oxidation. Sherry-style wine is the exception. These wines can be made from a variety of ingredients. They should be fermented with a sherry yeast and sugar should be fed into the must in the same way as for dessert wines. Great care should be taken when feeding a sherry-style must that you want to finish dry rather than sweet. Do ensure that the yeast has an adequate supply of nitrogen and vitamin B_1 and try your utmost to maintain an even temperature. Check the specific gravity every day or so and when 1.002 is reached, mix in quite small portions of sugar at a time, say 100g ($3\frac{1}{2}$ oz) per gallon. As the fermentation slows down, give the must a good stir to remove any bound carbon dioxide and to admit some fresh oxygen. Allow the specific gravity

reading to fall to 0.998 and increase it only to 1.002. Later let the reading fall to 0.996 and increase it only to 0.998. This constant addition of small quantities of sugar will slowly build up a high alcohol content with virtually no residual sugar.

After racking, mix in a bottle of commercial sherry of a similar style and then mature the wine for a year or two in a container not quite full (say only seven-eighths full), and plug the neck with cotton wool rather than a bung. As the wine swells and shrinks with the day to night temperature variations, some air will be pushed out and some fresh air will be drawn in. The cotton wool acts as a filter catching the micro-organisms floating in the air. The high alcohol content will also help to protect it.

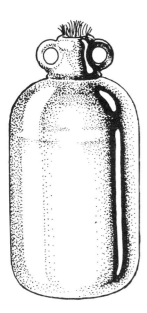

Sherry is essentially a blend of wines and it is a good idea to make several sherry-style wines and to blend them together. If possible, keep your sherry-style wine in such a container that as you draw off, say, a quarter of the total contents for bottling, the container can be topped up with similar style wine. It is rarely necessary to fortify a dry sherry-style wine with spirit, but an appropriate quantity of vodka may be added to a sweet sherry-style wine if you so wish. The distinctive sherry-style bouquet and flavour is obtained from suitable ingredients fermented with a sherry yeast to a high alcohol content, and then matured in the presence of air. The different alcohols combine with different acids to form aldehydes and fragrant esters of the sherry-style wine.

DESSERT WINES

Since these wines need to be well-flavoured and full-bodied, it is necessary to use a large quantity of the basic ingredient, as well as additional sugar to create the higher alcohol content, but, at the same time, great care must be taken not to kill the yeast by too much sugar. For this reason, it is best to feed in the sugar in smaller quantities. The recipes recommend the addition of three equal portions over a period of weekly intervals. A more precise way is to take frequent specific gravity readings and to stir the sugar into the must in even smaller portions each time the reading falls to, say, 1.002.

The occasional stir admits some oxygen and enables some cells to reproduce themselves, thus maintaining a strong yeast colony. Adequate nutrient in the form of di-ammonium phosphate and/or ammonium sulphate, together with some vitamin B_1 is necessary to maintain the activity of the yeast cells and their enzymes. An even temperature between 20–25°C (68–77°F) is also necessary.

The fermentation of so much sugar may take up to six weeks, but for the whole of the period that bubbles can be seen rising and heard bursting with a soft hissing sound, leave the must undisturbed. Only when fermentation is undoubtedly at an end should the new wine be racked from its sediment into a storage jar. If you so wish, three 5 ml teaspoonsfuls of glycerine per gallon may now be added to enhance the richness and smoothness of the wine. The sweetness should also be adjusted and the wine left alone in the dark for a year or two so that it can mature. Darkness is necessary to avoid fading of the wine by the light. Dessert wines do need long maturation and may not reach their peak for three or four years. Vintage port, it should be noted, needs a minimum of twelve years.

Fortification

In the eighteenth and nineteenth centuries it was common practice to add brandy to all wines, mainly because the techniques of fermentation as we now know them, were not then known. Too much sugar, insufficient acid and nutrient and the wrong yeast meant that only a small quantity of alcohol was produced by fermentation. The rest had to be added in the form of brandy. Today, spirits are never added to a wine unless to make it into a dessert wine.

With the method of fermentation described above, some 16% or 17% alcohol can often be obtained. If an even stronger wine is required, then it must be fortified with spirits. Brandy imparts its own unique flavour to a wine so we now use vodka which is both colourless and tasteless. As a rule of thumb, one bottle of vodka can increase the alcohol content of a gallon of wine by about 4%. More precise measurements can be obtained by using a Pearson's Square, thus:

$$A \qquad B$$
$$C$$
$$D \qquad E$$

In the corner marked A write the alcohol content of the wine to be fortified.

In the centre marked C write the alcohol content of the spirit to be used.

In the corner marked B write the alcohol content required in the fortified wine.

In the corner marked D write the difference between A and B.

In the corner marked E write the difference between A and C.

The ratio between D and E is the number of bottles of spirit required to raise the unfortified wine to the alcohol level required Thus:

Let $A = 14$ $B = 18$ $C = 40$
then $D = 4$ $E = 26$

Therefore 4 bottles of spirit are needed to increase the alcohol content of 26 bottles of the given wine to 18% alcohol by volume.

Experience shows that it takes some time for a spirit to be integrated into a wine. Preferably it should be done just before fermentation is finished, but at the latest it should be done as soon as the new wine is first racked from its lees. The fortified wine must then be left for at least one year to homogenise.

Fortification of flavour can be achieved by adding one bottle of certain commercial wines to home-made wines. Wines like Bulgarian Cabernet when added to a gallon of new red table wine impart an elegance of bouquet and flavour to the wine.

Similarly, a bottle of sherry added to a gallon of home-made sherry improves the bouquet and flavour considerably after a period of storage.

6 Country fruits and their wines

The following recipes are given for single-base ingredients. The addition of the small quantity of sultanas does not vary the flavour, but it does improve the fermentation and also enhances the vinosity of the wine. Fresh grapes may be used instead of the sultanas, or a bottle of pure grape juice, or some concentrated grape juice.

Throughout the recipes precise quantities are not critical. A little more or less will make no discernible difference. The quantity of water recommended can only be approximate and you may need a little more or even a little less to fill your jar. Glass demijohns have a nominal capacity of 4.5 litres (1 gallon) but some hold up to 4.8 litres (8½ pints). Even so, keep them full. All the recipes are designed to make 4.5 litres (1 gallon) (which is the equivalent of 6 standard wine bottles), unless otherwise stated. You can increase the quantity of wine made by increasing all the ingredients *pro rata* except the yeast which is sufficient for from one to five gallons.

APPLES

From the Bible we learn that Eve tempted Adam with an apple, and there is a lot of other evidence to indicate that the apple is one of the oldest fruits known to mankind. It is widely cultivated in all the temperate zones of the earth, especially in areas that are usually free from late spring frosts. Some 2,000 different varieties of apples have been identified and new ones continue to be hybridised. Apples are normally grown on trees, but there are some bush forms, dwarf forms, espalier trained, fan trained and cordon trained forms, all of which can produce excellent fruit in abundance.

The earliest apples ripen in the south of England in August, others come much later and some can be kept in a suitable store until the following April.

Home winemakers do not know which are the best varieties to use, although we do know that culinary varieties, such as the Bramley, contain too much acid and not enough flavour to make a good wine on their own. For those lucky enough to have access to sufficient quantity Cox's Orange Pippin makes an excellent base on which to build a balanced recipe.

Most of us use a mixture of eating and cooking apples and when possible add in a few crab apples or hard pears. A few quince can also enhance the bouquet and flavour. Indeed, the formula is not dissimilar from that given later for cider (see pp. 98–101). Whenever possible use 4 parts of mixed eating apples with 2 parts of mixed cooking apples and just 1 part of crab apples or hard green pears.

Country fruits and their wines

If you do not have access to such a range of apples at any one time, do not despair. Make up your wines from the different apples available to you throughout the season and blend them together in the following spring. In this way I have sometimes been able to include as many as 22 different varieties in my apple wine. Overall, however, do keep an eye on the balance and use plenty of tasty eating apples.

After the grape, a good eating apple contains more sugar than almost any other fruit, 13%. The cooking apple contains about two-thirds as much sugar but almost twice as much acid – malic, of course. Apple skin and pulp is as pectinous as the plum and an adequate quantity of a pectin-reducing enzyme must be included in the must. Apples contain a wide range of mineral salts and vitamins in modest quantities. It is rather low in nitrogen, however, and a half teaspoonful of an ammonium salt is recommended.

Apple wine is quite different from cider. Apart from being almost twice as strong, the wine often has a more delicate and refined flavour than the cider. It keeps well, sometimes taking two years to reach its plateau of perfection.

On a warm summer's evening, a bottle of cold apple wine shared between two people sat out in the garden can be just as enjoyable as a bottle of expensive German Moselle wine. Served with chicken, roast pork, baked ham, grilled fish or light-flavoured cheese, apple wine makes a splendid companion. A glass of apple wine used instead of water when stewing apples enhances their flavour significantly. Of all our country wines, only a few can match a well-made apple wine.

Apple table wine

Mixed eating apples	2 kg	4½ lb
Mixed cooking apples	1 kg	2¼ lb
Crab apples	500g	18 oz
Sultanas	250g	9 oz
Sugar	800g	1¾ lb
Water	2 l	3½ pt
Campden tablets		
Pectic enzyme		
Hock wine yeast and nutrient		

Apple dessert wine

Mixed eating apples	3 kg	6¾ lb
Mixed cooking apples	1 kg	2¼ lb
Crab apples	500g	18 oz
Sultanas	340g	12 oz
Sugar	1 kg	2¼ lb
Water	2 l	3½ pt
Campden tablets		
Pectic enzyme		
Sauternes wine yeast and nutrient		

Wash and finely crush the apples and drop them in a bin containing the water, the washed and chopped sultanas, pectic enzyme and one crushed Campden tablet. Cover and leave for 24 hours.

Stir in the nutrient and an activated wine yeast and ferment on the pulp for 7 days, keeping the pulp submerged, or gently pressed down twice each day.

Strain out, press dry and discard the pulp, stir in the sugar, pour the must into a demijohn and if needs be, top up with cold boiled water. Fit an airlock and ferment to a finish in an atmospheric temperature of about 16°C (61°F).

Rack into a storage jar, mix in some bentonite wine fining and one Campden tablet, seal and keep in as cold a place as possible until the wine is bright.

Rack again and store for a total of at least one year in bulk. Bottle and if needs be sweeten to taste before serving the wine nicely chilled.

NOTES

1 Because of their rather light flavour, apples are not suitable for making into a strong dessert wine.

2 The dry wine may be sparkled after six months (see pages 32–34).

3 Apples blend superbly well with all other fruits and you can enhance the flavours of most wines by including a few apples in the must.

Unsweetened apple juice from the grocer can also be used for making wine.

Apple juice wine

Unsweetened apple juice	2 l	3½ pt
Concentrated white grape juice	250g	9 oz
Sugar	680g	1½ lb
Water	2 l	3½ pt
Citric acid	10 ml	2 tsp
Pectic enzyme		
Campden tablets		
Hock wine yeast and nutrient		

Empty the apple juice into a demijohn, mix in the concentrated grape juice and two-thirds of the water. Add the acid, pectic enzyme and one crushed Campden tablet. Seal and leave in a warm place for 24 hours.

Dissolve the sugar in the rest of the water, add to the jar and then mix in the activated yeast and nutrient. Fit an airlock and ferment out in an atmospheric temperature around 15°C (59°F).

Rack into a storage jar, add one Campden tablet, seal and keep for six months before bottling.

Serve this wine cold at any time.

APRICOTS

Unfortunately, apricots are not widely grown in Britain, although they make a superb dry white wine. The tree is a native of China and it is thought that some young plants were given to Henry VIII in the sixteenth century, whose gardener planted them successfully. Apart from needing sun and warmth to ripen the fruit, as is the custom with many non-native trees, the tree presents two problems. The flowers often appear before sufficient insects are about to pollinate them and they need a warm and sheltered position if the fruit is to ripen properly. There are many gardens south of Nottingham where apricots can be, and sometimes are, grown as a fan-shaped tree spread over a south-facing wall. Moorpark is the most popular variety with its orange-coloured flesh and fine flavour.

The apricot contains as much acid as a cooking apple and the acid is three parts malic to one part citric. It is not very sweet, nor very pectinous although it is advisable to include a pectolytic enzyme in the must. The stone must be removed, of course, otherwise it will taint the wine.

Fresh apricots are often imported, mostly from Spain, but canned and dried apricots are also available. All make excellent wine. Dried apricots have a very intense flavour and it is recommended that not more than 500g per 5 litres be used. In small quantities, say 25g per litre, they make an excellent additive to other wines – red and white. They impart not only a subtle flavour but also some body and vitamins. Canned apricots, sometimes available as pieces in a wholesale pack, make a very fast-maturing wine that is sometimes ready to drink within three months. Apricot juice, usually described as apricot nectar, can also be bought and used to make wine.

Apricot table wine

Fresh apricots	2 kg	4½ lb
Sultanas	250g	9 oz
Sugar	800g	1¾ lb
Citric acid	5 ml	1 tsp
Grape tannin	2.5 ml	½ tsp
Water	4 l	7 pt
Pectic enzyme		
Campden tablets		
Burgundy wine yeast and nutrient		

Place the stalked, washed, stoned and crushed apricots in a bin containing the washed and chopped sultanas, the pectic enzyme, citric acid, one crushed Campden tablet and the water. Cover and leave for 24 hours.

Mix in the tannin and activated wine yeast and ferment on the pulp for 4 days, keeping the fruit submerged or gently pressed down twice each day.

Strain out, press dry and discard the pulp, stir in the sugar, pour the must into a demijohn, fit an airlock and ferment to dryness in a cool temperature, 15–16°C (59–61°F).

Rack into a storage jar, add one Campden tablet, seal and keep for one year before bottling.

Serve this dry white wine chilled with fish, poultry or pork.

Apricot social wine

Dried apricots	340g	12 oz
Sultanas	250g	9 oz
Sugar	1 kg	2¼ lb
Citric acid	10 ml	2 tsp
Water	4 l	7 pt
Pectic enzyme		
Campden tablets		
Sauternes wine yeast and nutrient		

Wash the dried apricots, then chop them up into small pieces. Place them in a bowl and pour 2 litres (3½ pints) of boiling water over them, cover and leave overnight.

Empty the apricots and steeping liquor into a bin, add the washed and chopped sultanas, the rest of the water, the pectic enzyme, citric acid and one crushed Campden tablet. Cover and leave for 24 hours, and continue as described for the fresh apricot wine.

It is probable that fermentation will stop before dryness is reached. Rack the wine and keep for one year, then serve it cool as a social wine.

BILBERRY

This attractive moorland shrub is called blaeberry, whortleberry and wimberry or whinberry, in different parts of the country. Its botanical name is *Vaccinium myrtillus* and so makes it a close relation of the better known blueberry (*Vaccinium corymbosum*) so popular in America as a pie filling. The bilberry is a little smaller than the blueberry, indeed it is more the size of a blackcurrant with an indentation at the free end. Like the blackcurrant, it is somewhat sharp if eaten raw, but its value for making into good red wine is outstanding.

It has a sugar content of about 6%, an acid content of about 1% (mostly citric but with some malic) and is rich in vitamins and mineral salts, other than potassium in which it is relatively low.

The knee-high shrub grows wild on heaths and moors over most of Britain, especially in the north but not in East Anglia. It can also be bought from garden centres for growing at home. For those who cannot get to the open country to gather these round, midnight-blue berries (not to be confused with the deadly nightshade) jars of bottled bilberries from Poland can be bought in some supermarkets and quality grocers.

Bilberries may be used by themselves to make a splendid red table wine, but their especial advantage is their contribution to colour and flavour when blended with blackberries or with apples. Even a few make a noticeable difference.

The fruits ripen from the end of July to the middle of September. They tend to hide under the inch-long pointed oval leaves and can be easily missed if not sought with considerable diligence.

Bilberry table wine 1

Fresh bilberries	2 kg	4½ lb
Concentrated red grape juice	250g	9 oz
Tartaric acid	5 ml	1 tsp
Grape tannin	5 ml	1 tsp
Sugar	900g	2 lb
Water	3.7 l	6½ pt
Pectic enzyme		
Campden tablet		
Burgundy wine yeast and nutrient		

Stalk, wash and crush the bilberries, place them in a bin and pour hot water over them, cover and leave to cool.

Stir in the acid, pectic enzyme and one crushed Campden tablet, then replace the cover and leave for 48 hours.

Strain out, press dry and discard the bilberries, mix in the concentrated grape juice, grape tannin and the activated yeast. Pour the must into a demijohn, leaving room for the sugar to be added after 5 days. Fit an airlock and ferment to dryness.

Rack into a storage jar, seal and keep for 18 months, then bottle and keep for a further 6 months.

Serve this dry red table wine free from chill with red meats and cheese.

Bilberry table wine 2

Bottled bilberries	900g	2 lb
Sultanas	250g	9 oz
Sugar	900g	2 lb
Citric acid	10 ml	2 tsp
Grape tannin	5 ml	1 tsp
Water	3.4 l	6 pt
Pectic enzyme		
Campden tablet		
Burgundy wine yeast and nutrient		

Open the jar, strain out the bilberries, save the syrup. Crush the bilberries and place them in a bin with the washed and chopped sultanas, the pectic enzyme, acid, one crushed Campden tablet and cold water. Cover and leave for 24 hours.

Mix in the syrup from the jar, the tannin and activated yeast, and ferment on the pulp for 4 days.

Strain out, press dry and discard the pulp, stir in the sugar, pour the must into a demijohn, fit an airlock and ferment to dryness.

Rack into a storage jar, seal and store for 6 months, then bottle and keep for another 3 months.

Serve free from chill as a dry red table wine at lunch time and with snacks.

BLACKBERRY

The blackberry must surely be our most prolific hedgerow fruit. It grows wild on railway embankments, along canals, country lanes, in open spaces, woodlands – wherever it can. The early and maincrop berries are often large and juicy with a good strong flavour. Unfortunately, the fruit is borne on thorny canes that often get tangled. This creates something of a problem when picking them, for hands and wrists are soon scratched all over, and trousers and jerseys suffer innumerable pulled threads.

Happily, the blackberry plant has been domesticated by our horticulturists and thornless versions may be bought, planted and trained on wires, walls or fences where the fruit can be gathered with ease. But you need a lot of blackberries to make all the red wine you would like to have. This can take several hours picking from the hedgerows. In the garden, fewer berries are likely to ripen at the same time and it may take several weeks to collect enough to make even six bottles of wine. As they are picked, the berries should be cleaned from their stalks and washed in a sulphite solution to remove hairs, tiny spiders, dust and the millions of invisible micro-organisms. After draining off the surplus moisture, the berries should be packed into suitable containers and frozen until required.

Blackberries are not quite so sweet as most other fruits, being comparable with the bilberry and gooseberry. They do have a good range of mineral salts and most vitamins except the important B_1, so necessary for a good fermentation; one 3 mg Benerva tablet should, therefore, be added to the must. Pectolytic enzyme should also be added since a fair amount of pectin is present – enough at least to make a good jam!

The acid content is comparable with cooking apples but is half malic and half citric. It would be sensible, then, only to add a little tartaric acid, preferably in the form of concentrated grape juice, sultanas or raisins.

The colour in blackberries can be leached out by pouring hot water over the crushed berries, followed by pulp fermentation, or by heating the crushed blackberries and water to 80°C (176°F) for 15 minutes. Be careful not to exceed this temperature, nor the time for which it is maintained. Cool the must as quickly as possible, strain out and press the pulp dry and use only the juice to make the wine.

Even so, the colour is not very deep and after a year or two in store – even in coloured bottles and stored in the dark – the original red fades to a tawny colour. This makes them a suitable ingredient on their own to make a tawny port-style wine but not for a full-blooded red table wine. Happily, blackberries blend superbly well with elderberries, bilberries, blackcurrants, damsons and black grapes. Some really fine red wines can be made by different combinations of these ingredients. Other combinations, such as blackberry and apple, are also very successful.

Blackberries are particularly subject to mould growth, especially after rain. Make a point of picking the fruit in dry weather and if possible in sunny conditions which many micro-organisms dislike. The difference in flavour between cultivated and hedgerow blackberries is not always distinguishable, although fruit gathered from the side of a busy road may well be tainted by the exhaust fumes of cars and lorries. Small berries growing on poor soil may be left for the birds, they are hardly worth the trouble of picking for wine. Use only the very best berries if you want to make really good wine.

Blackberry table wine

Cultivated blackberries	2 kg	4½ lb
Concentrated red grape juice	250g	9 oz
Sugar	800g	1¾ lb
Tannin	5 ml	1 tsp
Hot water	3.7 l	6½ pt
Pectic enzyme		
Campden tablets		
Burgundy wine yeast and nutrient		

No acid is required with blackberries.

Stalk, wash and crush the blackberries, place them in a bin and pour hot water over them. Cover and leave to cool, but give them a stir from time to time to aid extraction.

Add the pectic enzyme and one crushed Campden tablet and leave for 24 hours.

Strain out, press dry and discard the pulp, stir in the concentrated grape juice, tannin and an activated yeast. Pour the must into a demijohn, fit an airlock and ferment for 5 days.

Remove some must, stir in the sugar, return the must to the jar and ferment to dryness.

Rack into a storage jar, seal and store in total darkness for at least 1 year. Siphon into dark green or brown bottles and keep for another 3 months or longer.

Serve free from chill as a dry red table wine with red meats or cheese.

Alternative method

Cultivated blackberries	2 kg	4½ lb
Sultanas	250g	9 oz
Sugar	800g	1¾ lb
Cold water	4 l	7 pt
Tannin	5 ml	1 tsp
Pectic enzyme		
Campden tablet		
Burgundy wine yeast and nutrient		

Stalk, wash and crush the blackberries, add the washed and chopped sultanas, pour on the cold water, stir in the pectic enzyme and crushed Campden tablet, cover and leave for 24 hours.

Mix in the tannin and an activated yeast and ferment on the pulp for 4 days, keeping the blackberries submerged, or at least gently pressed down twice each day.

Strain out, press dry and discard the pulp. Stir in the sugar, pour the must into a demijohn and ferment to dryness.

Finish as already described.

Blackberry dessert wine

Wild blackberries	3 kg	6¾ lb
Sultanas	250g	9 oz
Sugar	1.36 kg	3 lb
Cold water	3.7 l	6½ pt
Tannin	5 ml	1 tsp
Pectic enzyme		
Campden tablet		
Port wine yeast and nutrient		

Stalk, wash and crush the blackberries, add the washed and chopped sultanas, pour on the cold water, stir in the pectic enzyme and crushed Campden tablet, cover and leave for 24 hours.

Mix in the tannin and the activated yeast, then ferment on the pulp for 4 days, keeping the fruit submerged or gently pressed down twice each day.

Strain out, press dry and discard the pulp, stir in one-third of the sugar, pour the must into a demijohn, fit an airlock and ferment for 1 week.

Remove some must, stir in half the remaining sugar, return this to the jar and continue the fermentation for another week.

Repeat this process and leave the must to finish fermenting.

Rack into a storage jar and keep in total darkness for at least 18 months. Siphon into dark green or brown bottles and store for a further 6 months or longer.

Serve this strong sweet wine after meals.
NOTES
1 Alternatively use the hot water method and concentrated grape juice as described in the Blackberry 1 recipe. Only 3.4 litres (6 pints) of water will be needed because of the concentrated grape juice.
2 Blackberries blend superbly with other fruits, notably the apple, elderberry and sloe.

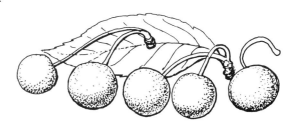

CHERRIES

There are two distinct and different kinds of cherries, both native to Britain. They are *Prunus arium* and *Prunus cerasus* – better known as sweet and sour! The sweet cherries grow on a large tree and need another nearby to pollinate it. The sour cherry on the other hand is self-fertile and grows on a much smaller tree or even one that is fan trained. For the best wine we need the sour cherries, although these are not always easy to obtain. Morello is the best known variety of sour cherry, but Kentish Red is equally successful.

Although called 'sour', these cherries contain only a moderate quantity of malic acid and a little citric. It is, therefore, important always to add some tartaric acid. They are low in pectin and so half the normal quantity of pectic enzyme is sufficient, but they are also low in nitrogenous material so nutrient in the form of ammonium phosphate must be added. The flavour of sour cherries is generally very strong, indicating a suitability for dessert wines.

Sweet cherries can be used but their flavour is less pronounced and you need something like 3 kg of sweet cherries to make six bottles of a dry table wine.

The cherry stones create an almond

flavour if left in the must, and cracked cherry stones could create a poisonous substance called cyanide. It is unlikely that sufficient will be formed to endanger health but the prudent winemaker will take the trouble to remove the stones with the stalks. In so doing, the fruit will be opened to allow the juice to run free.

Cherry wine

White sweet cherries	3 kg	6¾ lb
Sultanas	250g	9 oz
Sugar	680g	1½ lb
Tartaric acid	10 ml	2 tsp
Water	3.4 l	6 pt
Pectic enzyme		
Campden tablets		
Sauternes wine yeast and nutrient		

Stalk, wash and stone the cherries, crush or liquidise them. Add the washed and chopped or liquidised sultanas, the water, acid, pectic enzyme and one crushed Campden tablet. Cover and leave for 24 hours.

Mix in the activated yeast and nutrient, and ferment for 4 days, keeping the pulp submerged.

Strain out, press dry and discard the pulp, stir in the sugar, pour the must into a demijohn, fit an airlock and ferment out.

Rack into a storage jar, add one Campden tablet, seal and keep for 1 year before bottling. Serve this wine cold and sweetened to taste if so desired.

Cherry dessert wine

Black cherries	2.25 kg	5 lb
Sultanas	250g	9 oz
Sugar	1.25 kg	2¾ lb
Tartaric acid	10 ml	2 tsp
Tannin	5 ml	1 tsp
Water	2.84 l	5 pt
Pectic enzyme		
Campden tablets		
Port wine yeast and nutrient		

Stalk, wash, stone and crush the cherries and place them in a bin containing the washed and chopped sultanas, the water, the tartaric acid, pectic enzyme and one crushed Campden tablet. Cover and leave for 24 hours.

Mix in the tannin, activated yeast and nutrient and ferment for 4 days, keeping the fruit well submerged so as to extract as much colour as possible.

Strain out, press dry and discard the pulp, stir in half the sugar, pour the must into a demijohn, fit an airlock and ferment for 1 week. Stir in the rest of the sugar and ferment to a finish.

Rack into a storage jar, seal and keep for at least 1 year before bottling.

Serve free from chill as a sweet red dessert wine.

CRAB APPLES

The crab apple is the ancestor of the many eating and cooking varieties of apples which have been developed from it over the centuries. It grew, and grows, wild, although different varieties of crab apple trees can be bought from the larger garden centres. Nurserymen have improved on the original *Pyrus malus* by grafting, so that the fruit is now the size of a bantam's egg (John Downie), or of a golf ball (Dartmouth and Red Sentinel).

The fruit is rich in vitamins, organic acids (especially malic acid), and mineral salts. They have a bitter, sharp taste that puckers the mouth but make a splendid additive to cider and to apple wine. In Shakespeare's day some people used to roast crab apples and drop them into their ale for added flavour and nourishment.

When roasted crabs hiss in the bowl
Then nightly sings the staring owl . . .
(*Love's Labours Lost*, V.ii)

Spiced crab apples make an attractive accompaniment to roast pork and duckling, and need only a bottle of crab apple wine to make a perfect meal!

The John Downie variety of crab apple is a golden yellow with crimson patches. The fruits have stalks an inch long and grow in clusters for easy harvesting in September. They are the best variety for making wine (and jelly). I have grown and used this variety for many years, although I have made wine from other varieties as well. A fully grown John Downie tree will produce up to 20 pounds of fruit in a good year, enough to make 4 or 5 gallons of wine.

Crab apple wine

John Downie Crab apples	3 kg	6¾ lb
Sultanas	250g	9 oz
Sugar	800g	1¾ lb
Water	2.84 l	5 pt
Citric acid	5 ml	1 tsp
Pectic enzyme		
Campden tablets		
Sauternes wine yeast and nutrient		

Stalk, wash and crush the apples and drop them at once into a bin containing the water, the washed and chopped sultanas, the citric acid, one Campden tablet and the pectic enzyme. Cover and leave for 24 hours.

Mix in the activated wine yeast and nutrient and ferment on the pulp for 5 days, keeping the fruit submerged or at least gently pressed down twice each day.

Strain out, press dry and discard the pulp, stir in the sugar, pour the must into a demijohn, fit an airlock and ferment out.

Rack into a storage jar, add one Campden tablet and keep for 1 year before bottling.

Serve cold with cold meats and salads, snacks or cheese.

CURRANTS

Black, red and white currants all make good wine. The black is especially rich in mineral salts and vitamins, particularly vitamin C, of which it contains four times as much as lemons and five times as much as red- and whitecurrants. The blackcurrant also contains twice as much acid as the red- and whitecurrants, and almost as much as the lemon. The acid is mainly citric in all three currants but with a little malic and a trace of oxalic. The black also contains more sugar than the other two and also more pectin – the setting factor in jam. It is essential, then, to use a pectic enzyme when making blackcurrant wine.

Because of their very high acidity, blackcurrants should not be used at a rate of more than 1 kilogramme per 5 litres, or 2 pounds to the gallon. But such a small quantity of fruit on its own would produce a rather thin wine. A better alternative is to use only half this quantity of blackcurrants and make up the body with elderberries, bananas, dried apricots, prunes, sultanas, etc. Blackcurrants also blend well with eating apples and most other fruits, especially those lacking in flavour and acid.

Redcurrants make an attractive rosé wine that is particularly enjoyable at picnics and parties, with ham sandwiches, sausage rolls and paté.

Whitecurrants are much less abundantly available, but if you can find enough they should be used to make a sparkling wine.

Birds, particularly the attractive blackbirds and thrushes, adore currants of all kinds. They have an expert eye in recognising the perfect moment to eat them. Often they will beat you to the currants by a matter of hours! If you are growing currants, they certainly need protection. If you can, pick them when the flesh feels soft and the skin has a thin, almost translucent appearance. Clean them free from their stalks and wash them thoroughly in clean cold water containing one crushed Campden tablet and a similar quantity of citric acid. Drain them, crush them and use them at once, virtually straight from the bush. Like other soft fruit they quickly deteriorate once picked. If you cannot use them at once, pack them in a polythene box or thick polythene bag after washing them, seal securely and freeze them until required. They keep well over many months.

The unmistakable flavour of blackcurrants is also in the leaves of the bush. They can be gathered, washed and used for flavouring other wines, particularly vine and bramble prunings. A good handful is usually enough to add to any recipe for a gallon of wine. Blackcurrant leaves can also be frozen after washing and draining them. They can then be used when they would not otherwise be available.

Blackcurrant 'Port'

Blackcurrants	900g	2 lb
Bananas	450g	1 lb
Sultanas	250g	9 oz
Prunes	250g	9 oz
Sugar	1.25 kg	2¾ lb
Water	4 l	7 pt
Tannin	5 ml	1 tsp

Pectic enzyme
Campden tablet
Port wine yeast and nutrient
No acid is required.

Soak the prunes overnight in 1 litre (1¾ pints) hot water. Next day remove and discard the stones. Add the stalked, washed and crushed blackcurrants, the peeled and mashed bananas, the washed and chopped sultanas, the rest of the water (cold), the pectic enzyme and one crushed Campden tablet. Cover and leave in a warm place for 24 hours.

Mix in the tannin and activated wine yeast and ferment on the pulp for 4 days, keeping the fruit submerged or gently pressed down twice each day.

Strain out, press dry and discard the pulp, stir in approximately one-third of the sugar, pour the must into a fermentation jar, fit an airlock and ferment for 1 week.

Remove some must, stir in half the remaining sugar, and return this to the jar, replace the airlock and continue the fermentation. One week later, repeat this process with the remaining sugar and leave the fermentation to finish.

Rack into a clean jar, seal and store for 2 years in bulk, then bottle and keep for another 6 months.

Serve this strong, sweet, full-bodied wine after meals.

Redcurrant rosé

Redcurrants	900g	2 lb
Bananas	225g	½ lb
Sultanas	250g	9 oz
Sugar	900g	2 lb
Water	4 l	7 pt
Tannin	2.5 ml	½ tsp

Pectic enzyme
Campden tablets
Bordeaux wine yeast and nutrient
No acid is required.

Stalk, wash and crush the redcurrants and place them in a bin with the washed and chopped sultanas and the peeled and mashed bananas. Pour on tepid water (40°C/104°F), add the pectic enzyme and one crushed Campden tablet, then gently stir to mix all the ingredients together. Cover and leave for 24 hours.

Mix in the tannin and the activated wine yeast and ferment on the pulp for 4 days, keeping the fruit submerged or gently pressed down twice each day.

Strain out, press dry and discard the pulp, stir in the sugar, pour the must into a demijohn, fit an airlock and ferment out.

Rack into a storage jar, add one Campden tablet, seal and store for 9 months. Siphon into bottles adding one or at the most two saccharin pellets to each bottle. Cork, label and keep for a further 3 months.

Serve this wine cold at picnics or parties.

Whitecurrant sparkling wine

Whitecurrants	900g	2 lb
Sultanas	500g	18 oz
Sugar	600g	21 oz

Water	4 l	7 pt
Tartaric acid	5 ml	1 tsp
Tannin	2.5 ml	½ tsp
Pectic enzyme		
Campden tablet		
Champagne wine yeast		
Sugar	70g	2½ oz
Champagne wine yeast and nutrient		

Stalk, wash and crush the whitecurrants and place them in a bin containing the water, the washed and chopped sultanas, the tartaric acid, the pectic enzyme and one crushed Campden tablet. Stir gently, then cover and leave for 24 hours.

Mix in the tannin and the activated wine yeast and ferment on the pulp for 7 days, keeping the fruit submerged or pressed down twice daily.

Strain out, press dry and discard the pulp. Stir in the sugar, pour the must into a demijohn, top up if necessary, fit an airlock and ferment out in a temperature close to 15°C (59°F).

Rack through a filter into a storage vessel, seal and store for 6 months. Mix in the priming sugar (see pp. 33–34) and the new yeast, fit an airlock and when fermentation begins, siphon the wine into champagne bottles, seal with hollow domed stoppers and wire cages and lay the bottles on their sides. Leave them in a warm room for 6 days and a cool store for 6 months, then disgorge as described on pages 33–34.

DAMSONS

The damson is, of course, a member of the plum family, but it has such an individual flavour that it deserves a separate mention. It is the smallest fruit in the varied collection of plums and is notably distinct in colour and flavour. The tree is very hardy and self-fertile. It will grow in wet and exposed situations where other plums are difficult to grow and crop poorly. Indeed, the damson will succeed in places where gages will not

survive. This splendid vigour comes through in the fine flavour of the damson. In much the same way, the best wine grapes grow in soil not suitable for other crops.

The two best known varieties are Merryweather, producing a fleshy, black fruit in late August/early September; and Prune, producing a small, tapering, blue-black fruit in late September/early October. Left to itself the damson grows into a substantial tree, but it can be fan-trained or kept as a large bush.

The fruit grows on a stalk that is often attached to the stalks of other fruits in a similar way to cherries. They should be gathered by breaking off the main stalk protruding from the fruit bud of the tree. Picking at the fruit itself may damage it when fully ripe. It is not necessary to remove and discard each stalk, so that no woody taste is imparted to the wine, until you are ready to process the fruit into wine.

Damsons attract millions of micro-organisms that can be seen on their skin in the form of a whitish waxy bloom. This must be removed by washing the fruit for just a few minutes in hot water. Do not leave them so long as to cause the skins to split, but do remove any small globules of gum that you may occasionally find.

The fruit must then be opened and the stones removed. Because the fruit is so small this is a tedious task, but it is an important one. It is easier to do with fully ripe fruit, but do not include in the must any fruits that are over-ripe and have brown blemishes. It is best to use the fruit as fresh as possible and any fruits from which the stone cannot easily be removed should be placed in a basin and have hot water poured over them. By the time the water has cooled the fruit will be soft enough to enable you to extract and discard the stones. The flesh and water should then be added to the must.

Unlike other members of the plum family, damsons have an abundance of colour in their skins. This produces a rich red colour in the finished wine which is a joy to see.

Country fruits and their wines

Damsons are very tart and for this reason tend to make better dessert wines than table wines. The acid is mainly malic and imparts a fruity bouquet to the wine. Damsons are also very high in pectin – they make superb jam – and so the full measure of a pectic enzyme should be included. Damsons are rich in mineral salts and especially in vitamin B_1, but unlike most of our other fruits they contain no vitamin C.

Damson dessert wine

Stoned damsons	2 kg	4½ lb
Chopped raisins	500g	18 oz
White sugar	1 kg	2¼ lb
Water	3.4 l	6 pt
Pectic enzyme		
Campden tablet		
Port wine yeast		

No acid, tannin or nutrient is required.

Place the stoned and crushed damsons in a bin, add the washed and chopped raisins and pour on cold water. Mix in the pectic enzyme and one crushed Campden tablet. Cover and leave for 24 hours.

Stir in the activated yeast and ferment on the pulp for five days, keeping the fruit submerged or gently pressed down twice each day.

Strain out, press dry and discard the fruit, stir in one-third of the sugar, pour the must into a demijohn, fit an airlock and ferment in an even temperature of 20–21°C/68–70°F.

After one week, remove some must, stir in half the remaining sugar, return this to the jar and continue the fermentation.

One week later, repeat this process with the last portion of sugar, top up if necessary and ferment to a finish.

Rack the young wine into a storage vessel, check the specific gravity and if the reading is below 1.020, stir in sufficient sugar to make up the difference.

Mature this wine for at least two years before bottling, then keep it for a further six months before serving.

Damson table wine

Stoned damsons	1.5 kg	3½ lb
Raisins	250g	9 oz
Sugar	800g	1¾ lb
Water	4 l	7 pt
Pectic enzyme		
Campden tablet		
Burgundy wine yeast		

No acid, tannin or nutrient is required.

Place the stoned and crushed damsons in a bin, add the washed and chopped raisins and pour on cold water. Stir in the pectic enzyme and one crushed Campden tablet. Cover and leave for 24 hours.

Stir in the activated yeast and ferment on the pulp for only four days, keeping the fruit submerged or gently pressed down twice each day.

Strain out, press dry and discard the fruit, stir in all the sugar, pour the must into a demijohn, fit an airlock and ferment to a finish.

Rack the young wine into a storage vessel, top up and store for one year before bottling. Keep it a further six months and serve it free from chill with red meats or cheese.
NOTE:
Damsons blend well with other fruits, but do remember their high acidity: 450g (1 lb) of fruit in a gallon of wine contains 2 ppt of malic acid.

ELDERBERRY

This hedgerow tree or shrub, that produces creamy white flowers in summer and shiny black berries in autumn, is part of the folklore of many countries. It has been colloquially known as 'devil's tree', 'witch tree' and 'Judas' tree' – the latter because it was said to be the tree on which Judas hanged himself after betraying Jesus.

The elder used also to be called 'the country medicine chest', for all its parts had a use. The outer bark was used by Hippocrates to make a purgative, whilst the inner layer was used to make a soothing ointment. The

close-grained white wood was shaped and smoothed to make small items such as meat skewers, weaving needles, handles, etc. The stems were cleared of their soft centres and made into whistles and pop-guns. The leaves were infused to make a lotion that repelled mosquitoes and flies. It was also spread around plants to ward off caterpillars. The flower petals were used to make an infusion for soothing inflamed eyes and for fading freckles. Elderflower tea was an old remedy for influenza and was popular as a spring medicine, so often thought necessary by country folk. The flowers were also an active ingredient in an ointment that relieved the pain of chilblains, scalds and burns. Their use for making a delicious white wine is widely known.

The ripe berry was frequently used instead of currants in tarts, scones and cakes, as well as in jam, jelly, chutney and sauce. But best known of all is elderberry wine. It is usually made sweet and strong as the poor man's port, and was sometimes commercially mixed with port as a colour improver – a practice now forbidden.

Both the flowers and the berries can be dried and used the year round.

Elderberries are no lower in acid than many other fruits, containing upon average about 1%. It is mainly citric with a little malic. It is high in tannin, however, mostly in the skins. A wide range of vitamins and amino-acids are present which account for much of its nutritional value. The sugar content is not dissimilar from other wild fruits (8 to 10%).

But every winemaker knows that there are elderberries and elderberries! That is to say some are better than others! At least eight different varieties of *Sambuca nigra* have been identified but, alas, no research has yet been done to identify the most suitable varieties. The best advice that can be given is to use a mixture of all the different varieties that you can find. Some types have larger berries than others; some are globular in shape, others are slightly egg-shaped. Some hang from red stalks, others from green stalks. Move from bush to bush and gather the best drupes from each. A good drupe will be large with up to 100 berries, all of which will be a deep black and fully developed. The weight of the ripe fruit will cause the stem of the drupe to bend over so that the berries will all be hanging head down.

Gather only those drupes that are just fully ripe. Leave those with some green and unripe berries still showing and those that are clearly drying up and past their best. Cut the stem of the stalk with a knife and lay the drupe in a basket or similar container. As far as possible, spread them out so that the weight of the berries above does not crush the fruit beneath. The juice has a very strong colour and quickly stains every absorbent surface with which it comes into contact – including the hands. You may prefer to wear rubber gloves when handling elderberries.

Within an hour or two of picking the drupes, someone should be stripping off the berries. Combs and forks are sometimes used but they pull off the cap stems as well. The fingers are much more selective and sensitive. If the berries are not picked off without delay the stalks come with them making it much harder to clean them. After several days it is almost impossible to strip the berries cleanly from the drupes, and as there is plenty of tannin, and other phenolics, in the fruit itself, when pieces of cap stem and stalk are left in the bitter flavour becomes excessive and unpleasant.

The cleaned berries, then, should all be whole, large, black and free from every trace of leaf, stem and stalk. They should now be placed in a colander and rinsed in running cold water to remove traces of dust, tiny flies, spiders and even earwigs. Shake off the surplus moisture and place them in a polythene bin. Crush them with a potato masher or some similar instrument so that each berry is broken. Pour freshly boiled water over them, cover and leave to cool.

The crushing releases the juice and the hot water assists in the extraction of the colour and other constituents. The old method of boiling the fruit until it dimpled extracted too much bitterness. Cold water fails to extract sufficient colour.

When the fruit juice and water has cooled to about 20°C (68°F), strain the berries through a fine-meshed nylon sieve and press them dry. Stir up the pulp from time to time during the pressing so that all the berries are equally pressed.

The juice is now ready for fermenting with concentrated grape juice, washed and chopped sultanas or raisins, freshly crushed grapes or just with sugar and lemon juice or citric acid.

The quantity of berries to use is largely a matter of taste and time. Some people do not enjoy the elderberry flavour and blend the berries with other fruit, such as blackberries, damsons, sloes, apples and so on. For them, 1 kg (2 lb) in the 5 litres (1 gallon) is sufficient to make a well-flavoured dry red table wine. Rather more may be used in a sweet dessert wine. Other people, however, enjoy this robust country flavour, using 2 kg (4½ lb), and with the patience of a countryman, are willing to leave their wine for four or five years to mature. During this time the harshness is ameliorated and a softer, fuller wine is produced. The following recipes take account of both views and different styles of wine.

Elderberry dessert wine

Freshly picked elderberries	2 kg	4½ lb
Sugar	1.5 kg	3½ lb
Water	3.4 l	6 pt
Fresh lemon	1	
Port wine yeast and nutrient		

No tannin needed.

Stalk, wash, drain and crush the elderberries, add the thinly pared and chopped yellow lemon skin, pour hot water over them, cover and leave to cool.

Strain out, press dry and discard the pulp; stir in the expressed and strained juice of the lemon, half the sugar and the activated wine yeast.

Pour the must into a demijohn, fit an airlock and ferment for ten days.

Remove some must, stir in the rest of the sugar, return this to the jar, top up and ferment to a finish.

Rack into a storage jar, seal and store for two years. Bottle, sweeten to taste with saccharin, and serve after meals.

A teaspoonful of glycerine per bottle imparts a rich smoothness to the wine.

Elderberry table wine

Elderberries blend very well with other autumn fruits to make a dry red table wine.

Freshly picked elderberries	680g	1½ lb
Freshly picked blackberries	1 kg	2¼ lb
Freshly picked damsons/sloes	340g	12 oz
Concentrated red grape juice	250g	9 oz
Sugar	900g	2 lb
Citric acid	5 ml	1 tsp
Water	3.4 l	6 pt
Burgundy wine yeast and nutrient		

Stalk, wash, crush and stone the fruit, pour hot water over it, cover and leave to cool. Strain out, press dry and discard the pulp, stir in the concentrated grape juice, the acid and the activated yeast.

Pour the must into a demijohn, fit an airlock and ferment for four days.

Remove some must, stir in the sugar, return this to the jar and ferment out.

Rack into a storage jar, seal and store in a cool place for two years.

Serve free from chill with meat or cheese.
NOTE
The quantities given are not critical and may be varied to suit the fruits available.

Dried elderberry wine
Dried elderberries may be bought if you cannot obtain any fresh elderberries.

Dried elderberries	450g	1 lb
Concentrated red grape		
juice	250g	9 oz
Sugar	900g	2 lb
Citric acid	10 ml	2 tsp
Water	4 l	7 pt
Burgundy wine yeast and nutrient		

Wash the berries in a sulphite solution and remove as many stalks as you can.

Boil the berries for 20 minutes in as much of the water as you can manage in a covered pan, then leave them to cool.

Strain out, press dry and discard the berries. Mix in the concentrated grape juice, the citric acid and the activated yeast. Pour the must into a demijohn then continue as for elderberry table wine.

Elderflower social wine
Freshly picked		
elderflowers	560 ml	1 pint
Sultanas	500g	18 oz
Sugar	500g	18 oz
Citric acid	5 ml	1 tsp
Water	4.25 l	7½ pt
Hock wine yeast and nutrient		
Campden tablet		

Remove every trace of stalk and stem and place the florets in a suitable vessel. Pour on hot water, macerate the florets against the side of the vessel with the back of a plastic spoon, cover and leave to cool.

Add the washed and chopped sultanas, the citric acid and the active yeast. Ferment on the pulp for three days, keeping the pulp submerged, or gently pressed down twice each day.

Strain out the pulp, stir in the sugar, pour the must into a demijohn, fit an airlock and ferment out.

Rack into a storage jar, add one Campden tablet and keep for six months.

Bottle, sweeten to taste with saccharin and serve cold as a summer social wine.

GOOSEBERRIES

Although a native shrub of northern Europe, the gooseberry is only popular in the United Kingdom. Here it is grown widely and different varieties have been developed since Tudor times. Dessert varieties such as Golden Drop and Langley Gage are for eating fresh from the bush. Red varieties, such as Keepsake and Warrington may be used either for cooking while green or eating as a dessert when fully ripe. Several other varieties are grown for cooking in one way or another in tarts, pies, fools and jams.

The gooseberry makes some of the very best country wines and could well be described as the Englishman's grape! The author's favourite variety is Careless, a mid-season green gooseberry that crops generously with large fruits. It makes a fine light dry table wine, extraordinarily reminiscent of a good German Hock. It can also be used to make a splendid sparkling wine. Another green variety that makes a good wine is Leveller. The wine is fuller and if fermented with a Sauternes wine yeast, produces a rich sweet table wine.

These two varieties of gooseberry contain little sugar but a good quantity of a 50/50 mixture of citric and malic acid. They have a high pectin content, so a pectic enzyme should always be added to the must. Some winemakers remove the stem and flower before using the gooseberry, but this is not essential. It is important, however, to wash them thoroughly in a weak sulphite solution. In spite of being harvested when fully grown and mature, these gooseberries are not easy to crush. One way is to pour hot water over them and leave them to cool. The berries are then much softer and can be crushed between the fingers or in a liquidiser.

Gooseberries freeze very well. After cleaning and washing them, drain them and pack them into polythene boxes or good-quality polythene bags, seal them securely and store them in your freezer until required.

Gooseberry table wine

Careless gooseberries	1.25 kg	3 lb
Sultanas	250g	9 oz
Sugar	800g	1¾ lb
Water	4 l	7 pt
Tartaric acid	5 ml	1 tsp
Pectic enzyme		
Campden tablets		
Hock wine yeast		
Vitamin B_1	3 mg	1 tablet

Gooseberry sparkling wine

Careless gooseberries	1 kg	2¼ lb
Sultanas	250g	9 oz
Sugar	800g	1¾ lb
Water	4 l	7 pt
Tartaric acid	5 ml	1 tsp
Pectic enzyme		
Campden tablet		
Champagne wine yeast		
Vitamin B_1	3 mg tablet	
Champagne wine yeast		
Sugar	70g	2½ oz
Nutrient	2.5g	½ tsp

Gooseberry dessert wine

Leveller gooseberries	1.5 kg	3½ lb
Sultanas	250g	9 oz
Sugar	1 kg	2¼ lb
Water	3.7 l	6½ pt

Tartaric acid	5 ml	1 tsp
Pectic enzyme		
Campden tablets		
Sauternes wine yeast		
Vitamin B_1	3 mg	1 tablet

Wash the gooseberries, crush them, add the washed and chopped sultanas, the pectic enzyme, acid and one crushed Campden tablet. Cover and leave for 24 hours.

Mix in the activated wine yeast and nutrient and ferment on the pulp for three days, keeping the fruit submerged or gently pressed down twice each day.

Strain out, press dry and discard the pulp, stir in the sugar, pour the must into a demijohn, fit an airlock and ferment to a finish.

Rack into a storage jar, add one Campden tablet in recipes 1 and 3, but not in 2; seal; store wines 1 and 3 for one year and wine 2 for six months.

For wine 2, add the priming sugar, nutrient and second yeast, fit an airlock and when the wine is fermenting, pour into champagne bottles and seal with hollow-domed stoppers and wire cages. Lay the bottles on their side for 1 week in a warm room and then a cool store for 6 months.

GRAPE

The vine has provided both food and drink for mankind for some 10,000 years – certainly since Noah planted his vineyard after the Flood. Fresh and dried grapes were a source of summer and winter food respectively. Wine made from the juice was drunk through the winter and spring.

The Romans are most likely to have brought the vine (*Vitis vinifera*) to Britain. It had long been grown in Italy and the soldiers and settlers stationed in Britain grew the vine as best they could in our less clement weather. One of the varieties at present being grown in some of the many small vineyards that are being developed is the Wrotham Pinot, thought to have been brought to England by Julius Caesar.

But the vine did not flourish along the banks of the Thames as it did along the banks of the Mosel and the Rhine, the Loire, the Saône and the Garonne. A few vines survived under glass or against south-facing walls in sheltered places, but we have always been an importer of wine.

Since the 1960s, however, new efforts have been made to grow vines based on new varieties and better viticulture. Hundreds of thousands of gardeners now grow at least a few vines, especially in the South of England where there are also several hundred vineyards producing wine commercially. The most popular varieties of grape vines are Muller-Thurgau, Seyval, Madeleine Angevine, Siegerebe and Seibel, but experiments are also being made with many new varieties. In general, the white grapes are most likely to ripen, but even in a good summer they are likely to be high in acid and low in sugar.

Wine made from the juice of the grape has been referred to as 'a chemical symphony composed of ethyl alcohol, several other alcohols, sugar, other carbohydrates, polyphenols, aldehydes, ketones, enzymes, pigments, at least half a dozen vitamins, fifteen to twenty minerals, more than twenty-two organic acids, and other grace notes that have not yet been identified.' Nearly 400 components have already been isolated, and the possible variations in composition are infinite, depending on the variations in grape variety, climate, soil and the different processes of viticulture and vinification of the grape juice.

Grapes should not be picked before the flesh has softened and there is a translucent appearance in the skin. Weather and birds permitting, they may be left on the vine as long as possible so that the acid decreases and the sugar increases.

Few grape varieties make superb wine by themselves and many of the great wines of the world contain a blend of several varieties. It is worthwhile, then, to grow several varieties from which to make wine.

After cutting the bunches from the vines,

rinse them in a sulphite solution, not only to inhibit the growth of micro-organisms but also to remove dust and insects.

White wine

Crush the clean grapes, then remove and discard the stems. Strain off, through fine meshed nylon, sufficient juice to enable you to check its specific gravity. A white wine needs to have an original reading of between 1.076 and 1.082. If the reading is below this, you should calculate how much sugar to add to raise the reading appropriately: 56g (2 oz) sugar added to 4.5 litres (1 gallon) of must raises the reading by about 5 points. Do not add the sugar at this stage but add instead one crushed Campden tablet and one 5 ml spoonful of a pectic enzyme per gallon. Cover the must and leave it for 24 hours, then strain out, press quite dry and discard the skins and pips. Some winemakers advocate the immediate pressing of the pulp, but in my opinion, the grape aroma in the finished wine is enhanced by the short period of contact between skin and juice.

After pressing, the additional sugar together with an activated wine yeast should be mixed into the juice and the must should be poured into demijohns and airlocks fitted. As soon as fermentation starts, move the jars to a cool place where the atmospheric temperature is no more than 15°C (59°F). Fermentation will be slow and may take up

to six weeks but the resulting wine will be better flavoured.

When fermentation finishes and the wine begins to clear, siphon the wine through a filter into sterilised jars containing one crushed Campden tablet per gallon to prevent oxidation and infection. Fill each jar to the bung and seal securely, label and store in a cool place for six months before bottling. If at this stage the wine tastes too dry, sweeten it slightly with liquid saccharin at the rate of two or three drops per bottle.

Red wine

If you have a sufficient crop of black grapes (you need at least 8 kg (18 lbs) to make six bottles of wine), wash them in a sulphite solution, crush them and remove the stalks, strain out enough of the juice to check the specific gravity and calculate how much sugar must be added to raise the reading to 1.090. Mix in the sugar and when completely dissolved add pectic enzyme and an activated wine yeast. Cover the vessel and ferment the must on the pulp for eight to ten days until the colour is dark enough. Keep the floating cap of skins and pips well pressed down, at least twice each day. This ensures a better extraction and prevents infection of the cap. Strain out, press dry, and discard the skins. Finish the fermentation under an airlock.

Dr Chris Somers of the Australian Wine Research Institute in Adelaide has developed an alternative method of extracting the colour and other constituents from black grapes. As soon as the grapes are crushed and the stalks removed, heat the must as quickly as you can in a covered vessel until the temperature reaches 80°C (176°F) – no more. Do not let the must boil or a cooked fruit flavour may develop in the wine. Hold the temperature at 80°C for 15 minutes, then remove the vessel from the stove and cool the must, again as quickly as you can, by, e.g. spraying cold water over the vessel.

As soon as the temperature has fallen to 20°C (68°F), strain out the skins and pips, press them quite dry and discard them. Check the specific gravity of the must and, if necessary, stir in sufficient sugar to increase the reading to 1.090. Add pectic enzyme and an activated wine yeast, pour the must into demijohns and fit airlocks. Ferment in an atmospheric temperature of about 20°C (68°F) until activity ceases. Mix in some wine finings and leave the wine in a cold place for about one week while the wine clears. Siphon the clear wine into storage jars, bung tight, label and leave the wine to mature in a cool place. Because of the high acid content of English-grown grapes, this wine may take several years to mature. If stored in a cold place some of the tartaric acid may precipitate as potassium tartrate (glass-like crystals). Furthermore, if no sulphite is added, some of the malic acid may be converted into the less sharp lactic acid. Both these processes aid the maturation of the wine.

Rosé wine

This is normally made from black grapes that are left fermenting on their skins for a day or so until the juice has become a pretty pink. The skins are then removed, pressed and discarded (or added to a plum must). Fermentation of the pink juice is then conducted as for a white wine.

Vinefolly wine

In the summer, the vine shoots grow vigorously and must be pruned if the fruit is to be developed. Once the flowers have set and tiny bunches of grapes have appeared, remove all the growth beyond the second leaf after the bunch of fruit. Unwanted side shoots from the main stem should also be removed. Several vines produce quite a pile of these prunings. They can be washed, chopped and made into quite an attractive light white wine. The flavour can be enhanced by a few handfuls of blackcurrant leaves.

Prunings and leaves	3 kg	6¾ lb
Concentrated white grape juice	250g	9 oz
or		
Pure grape juice	560 ml	1 pt
Sugar	800g	1¾ lb
Tartaric acid	15 ml	3 tsp
Water	3.69 l	6½ pt
Wine yeast		

Chop the washed prunings and leaves into small pieces, place them in a large pan with the water, heat to 80°C (176°F), hold this for 15 minutes, then cool, strain out and press the leaves dry before discarding them.

Stir in the grape juice, acid, sugar and the activated yeast. Pour the must into a fermentation jar, fit an airlock and leave in a cool place (17°C/62°F) until activity ceases.

Siphon the wine through a filter, add one Campden tablet per gallon, seal the jar, label and store for six months before bottling.

NOTE

Washed and chopped prunings may be packed into polythene bags, pressed flat, sealed and stored for future use. They make a useful additive to any wine.

Similarly with grapes. If in a poor season you have insufficient to make wine from them exclusively, they may be crushed and added to any other must. If you have no other must available for them at the time, wash and crush them, remove the stalks, pack the pulp and juice into polythene boxes or bags, seal them securely and freeze them until required. One kilo of fresh or frozen grapes is the equivalent of 250g sultanas.

DRIED GRAPES

Dried grapes have been an item of trade for at least 3,000 years and have been imported into London for many centuries. The centre of this trade has always been in Cheapside. In 1635 King Charles I granted a licence to Francis Chamberlayne permitting him to make and sell wine from 'raysons'. They have been used ever since as an important additive to country wines and raisin wine has remained as popular as ever.

Sultanas, as we know them today, are usually made from seedless white grapes and raisins from the seedless Thompson grape. True raisins, however, are those containing a seed. In preparing wine from them you must be careful to break open the flesh without crushing or damaging the seed, for this would impart an unpleasant flavour to the wine.

Sultanas and raisins lose some of their acid in the drying process but retain their wealth of minerals, vitamins and amino-acids. Approximately two-thirds of their weight consists of fermentable sugars, thus 500g (18 oz) sultanas or raisins contain approximately 340g (12 oz) sugar. When using sultanas in your own recipes this sugar content must be included in the total. 250g (9 oz) of sultanas or raisins contain approximately 0.1% acid equal to 1 part per thousand in a gallon of must. The fruit is well supplied with nitrogenous material. One measure of dried fruit is the equivalent of four measures of fresh fruit. Accordingly, some 2 kg (4½ lb) sultanas or raisins will be needed to make six bottles of wine.

Dried grape wine

Sultanas/raisins	2 kg	4½ lb
Water	4.5 l	1 gal
Citric acid	5 ml	1 tsp
Sauternes wine yeast		
Campden tablet		

Wash and chop the fruit, then place in a bin with the acid and water. Add the active yeast and ferment on the pulp for ten days, keeping the fruit submerged the whole time. Strain out, press dry and discard the fruit, pour the must into a demijohn, fit an airlock and ferment to a finish.

Rack into a storage jar, add one Campden tablet, seal and store for one year. Serve cold with fruit cake.

LOGANBERRY

This plant first appeared in the USA about a century ago as a result of a cross between a blackberry and a raspberry. The new fruit is larger than both its parents, almost twice as sharp and a little less sweet. It has a fine but pronounced flavour and is best suited for dessert wines. It is unlikely to be found growing wild. It is best grown on a sunny fence attached to wires about 12 inches apart. The plant is quite vigorous and the fruit appears on the previous year's canes. As with raspberries, the fruiting cane should be cut off at ground level as soon as the harvest is completed. The wine is a light red colour.

Incidentally, the name loganberry was bestowed on the fruit by Judge Logan in 1881 who successfully crossed the blackberry and raspberry.

Loganberry dessert wine

Loganberries	1.8 kg	4 lb
Dried apricots	125g	4½ oz
Sultanas	250g	9 oz
Bananas	250g	9 oz
Sugar	1.35 kg	3 lb
Water	3.7 l	6½ pt
Tannin	5 ml	1 tsp
Pectic enzyme		
Campden tablet		
Tokay yeast		
No acid needed.		

Stalk, wash and crush the loganberries, wash and chop the dried apricots and sultanas, peel and mash the bananas; pour on cold water, add the pectic enzyme and one crushed Campden tablet, stir well, cover and leave for 24 hours in a warm place.

Add the tannin and the activated Tokay yeast and ferment on the pulp for four days, keeping the fruit submerged or gently pressed down twice each day.

Strain out, press dry and discard the pulp, stir in one-third of the sugar, pour the must into a demijohn, fit an airlock and ferment in a warm place for one week.

Remove some of the must, stir in half the remaining sugar, then return this to the jar. One week later add the remaining sugar in the same way, then leave to finish fermenting.

Rack the new wine from its sediment, seal and store for at least two years.

This is a sweet and strong dessert wine with a pronounced flavour. Serve it after meals.

NOTE

The apricots and bananas not only ameliorate the strong flavour of the loganberries but also add body to the wine. Loganberries may be added to other red musts to improve their flavour.

MEDLARS

Like the mulberry, the medlar is somewhat out of fashion in our modern world. Indeed, its shape and colour has a kind of old-world charm about it. The tree can sometimes be found on a roadside or in the garden of an old house. But the tree can also be bought from a good nurseryman and the variety to ask for is Nottingham. It is smaller than Dutch which has wide spreading branches and takes up too much space. Even so, you can expect a medlar tree to grow to about 5 metres high, so plant it well away from the house. The branches are gnarled and twisted and bear large pinky-white flowers in early summer. In autumn, the leaves become a brilliant russet-gold and the fruits are ready for picking. Lay them in a single layer, stalk up, in a cool store for three or four weeks to mellow. The skin turns a dark brown and the

flesh softens. The tomato-size fruit may then be eaten raw but can also be made into an attractive wine.

Medlar social wine

Ripe medlars	4 kg	9 lb
Sultanas	250g	9 oz
Sugar	1 kg	2¼ lb
Water	3.4 l	6 pt
Citric acid	5 ml	1 tsp
Grape tannin	2.5 ml	½ tsp
Pectic enzyme		
Campden tablets		
Sauternes wine yeast and nutrient		

Wash and crush the medlars and drop them into a bin containing the water, the washed and chopped sultanas, the pectic enzyme, citric acid and one crushed Campden tablet. Cover and leave for 24 hours.

Stir in the activated yeast, the tannin and nutrient, and ferment on the pulp for five days, keeping the fruit submerged, or gently pressed down twice each day.

Strain out, press dry and discard the pulp, stir in the sugar, pour the must into a demijohn, fit an airlock and ferment to a finish.

Rack into a clean jar, add one Campden tablet, seal and store for one year. Bottle and keep for some months longer.

Serve this wine cold as a social wine.

MULBERRY

The leaves of the mulberry tree (*Morus nigra*) are the sole food of silkworms and so you will often find these trees where silk was spun. The first mulberry tree was planted at Syon House, Brentford, in 1548 and James I planted one in the gardens of Buckingham Palace in 1610. The tree grows slowly and lives a very long time, but young trees can be bought. Of the two varieties – black and white – choose the black because this produces the best-flavoured fruit.

The mulberry looks rather like a large loganberry but has a dark, reddish-purple

hue. It has a pronounced flavour and is best used to make a dessert wine. When the first ripe fruits begin to fall from the tree, spread a cloth or paper or sheet of polythene all around from the bole to the limit of the branches. Gently shake the tree and its individual branches to encourage other ripe fruits to fall. It is important to use fully ripe fruit. Gather these, wash them in a weak sulphite solution, drain them, and freeze them until you have sufficient to make as much wine as you wish. Repeat the tree shaking each day until all the fruit has been gathered. Birds are extremely fond of mulberries and will certainly get some of your crop. Ripe mulberries contain approximately 8% sugar and 0.5% acid.

Mulberry wine

Ripe mulberries	2 kg	4½ lb
Sultanas	250g	9 oz
Water	3.4 l	6 pt
Tartaric acid	15g	½ oz
Vitamin B_1	3 mg	1 tablet
Sugar	1.25 kg	2¾ lb
Nutrient	5g	1 tsp
Tannin	2.5g	½ tsp
Port wine yeast		
Pectic enzyme		
Campden tablet		

Crush the mulberries, wash and chop the sultanas and place them in a bin, pour 2.84 litres (5 pints) hot water over them, cover

and leave to cool. Add the pectic enzyme, tartaric acid, one crushed Campden tablet and leave in a warm room for 24 hours.

Activate the wine yeast, mix in the nutrient and one crushed 3 mg Benerva tablet (vitamin B_1). Stir this into the pulp and ferment for 3 days, pressing down the fruit cap twice each day. Meanwhile, dissolve the sugar in (1 pint of) hot water.

Strain out, press dry and discard the pulp, stir in half the sugar syrup and continue the fermentation under airlock for 10 days.

Stir in the rest of the syrup and ferment to a finish.

When the wine begins to clear, move the jar to a cold place for 5 days, then rack the wine into a storage jar. Top up, seal and store until the wine is bright, then rack again and store for two years. Bottle and keep this wine for another year while the strong flavour ameliorates and the wine becomes smooth.

Taste the wine and, if needs be, sweeten it to suit your palate, then serve with Stilton cheese and biscuits.

NOTES

If you are a purist, the sultanas may be omitted but in the author's view it is a mistake to do so. The sultanas contribute about 6 oz sugar, a little acid and a mixture of minerals, vitamins and trace elements beneficial both to the fermentation and to the finished wine.

An alternative to sultanas is concentrated grape juice (250g/9 oz red). If this is used it should be added just before the yeast.

ORANGES

Although not indigenous to the English countryside, oranges, so closely associated with Nell Gwynne and Charles II, have long been a popular ingredient with country winemakers. The many varieties available in the UK come mainly from Spain and North Africa, but also from Israel and South Africa and other warm countries. The main acid in oranges is, of course, citric and there is a

good measure of vitamin C, as well as some fruit sugar.

Most of the flavour is in the coloured skin and this must be pared off very finely with a sharp potato knife. The white pith is very pectinous and also imparts a bitter taste, if included in the wine, that most people find unpleasant. After removing the very thin skin, the orange should be cut into halves across the segments and the juice squeezed out and strained through a fine nylon sieve. Use only the skin and juice to make the wine and discard all the rest.

The best orange wine seems to be made from a mixture of sweet and bitter oranges available at the end of January or the beginning of February, but other types can also be used.

Finely pared orange skin and strained juice may be added to a variety of wines to enhance their flavour and increase their acidity.

Canned or cartoned unsweetened orange juice, available from the grocer, may also be used to make wine.

Orange wine

Sweet oranges	6	
Bitter oranges	4	
Sultanas	250g	9 oz
Sugar	900g	2 lb
Water	4 l	7 pt
Pectic enzyme		
Campden tablets		
Sauternes yeast and nutrient		
Glycerine	15 ml	3 tsp

Wipe over the oranges with a cloth that has been dipped in a sulphite solution, thinly pare them and place the parings on a tray in a cooling oven for about 20 minutes.

Chop them up and place them in a bin with the washed and chopped sultanas, the pectic enzyme, one crushed Campden tablet, the water and the juice from the oranges. Cover and leave for 24 hours.

Add the activated yeast and nutrient and ferment on the pulp for four days, keeping the fruit cap well pressed down.

Strain out, press dry and discard the pulp, stir in the sugar, pour the must into a demijohn, fit an airlock and ferment to a finish.

Rack into a storage jar, add the glycerine and one Campden tablet, seal and store for one year.

Serve this wine cold with roast duck or as an aperitif.

Orange-juice wine

Unsweetened orange juice	2 l	3½ pt
Concentrated white grape juice	250g	9 oz
Sugar	900g	2 lb
Water	1.7 l	3 pt
Pectic enzyme		
Campden tablets		
Sauternes wine yeast and nutrient		

Empty the orange juice into a demijohn, add the concentrated grape juice, dissolve the sugar in the water and pour this into the demijohn. Add the pectic enzyme and one Campden tablet, seal the jar and leave for 24 hours. Mix in the activated yeast and nutrient, fit an airlock and continue as described above.

PEACHES AND NECTARINES

A Frenchman is said to have remarked that if peaches were as prolific as grapes, he would prefer to make his wine from them! Be that as it may, the peach and the nectarine (a smooth-skinned peach) are deservedly very popular for their delicious flavour. They make superb wine, especially sweet wine to accompany the dessert course of a meal. Given a warm and sheltered position, the peach tree flourishes in the south of Britain and also in suitable places in the north.

Like the apricot, the peach tree originated in China where it grows wild, and must have been taken to Persia during the period of the Great Empire. From there the tree was brought westwards, probably by the Romans, in the belief that it had originated in Persia – for its botanical name is *Prunus Persica*. The tree flourished in Rome and its surrounding country, and is likely to have been brought on to Britain to be planted in the gardens of the Roman villas.

The peach was grown in England long before the Norman invasion of 1066 because we know that the Anglo-Saxon name for the peach was Perseoctreou, meaning Tree of Persia.

Modern horticulturists have developed new varieties of which Peregrine is perhaps the best known. The fruit is only half as acidic as the apricot and, therefore, tastes sweeter although it contains very little more

sugar. It contains a good range of vitamins, mineral salts and nitrogenous substances and not too much pectin, all good indications of its suitability for making wine. The skin contains a bitter substance and is therefore best removed at the same time as the stone. Use fully ripe but not over-ripe or damaged fruit, and always include some tartaric acid. A minimum of 2 kg (4½ lb) of prepared fruit (i.e. minus skin and stones) is needed to make six bottles of wine.

Peach dessert wine

Peaches	2.5 kg	5½ lb
Sultanas	250g	9 oz
Tartaric acid	15 ml	3 tsp
Tannin	2.5 ml	½ tsp
Sugar	1 kg	2¼ lb
Water	4 l	7 pt
Pectic enzyme		
Campden tablets		
Sauternes wine yeast and nutrient		
Potassium sorbate	1g	¼ tsp

Peel, stone and crush the peaches, wash and chop the sultanas, pour on cold water, then gently stir in the acid, pectic enzyme and one crushed Campden tablet. Cover and leave for 24 hours.

Add the tannin, activated yeast and nutrient, and ferment on the pulp for 4 days, keeping the fruit well submerged.

Strain out the solids through a nylon bag, roll them around or press gently, and then discard them. Stir in the sugar, pour the must into a demijohn, fit an airlock and ferment down to specific gravity of 1.010 or just over.

Rack through a filter into a storage jar containing one crushed Campden tablet and one gram of potassium sorbate, or a crushed Sorbistat tablet. Seal the jar and keep in a cool place for one year.

Serve cold with the dessert course of a meal, or with sweet biscuits.

NOTE

The same recipe may be used for nectarines.

Pear sparkling wine

Hard green pears	3 kg	6¾ lb
Sultanas	170g	6 oz
Sugar	450g	1 lb
Water	2.8 l	5 pt
Tartaric acid	10 ml	2 tsp
Pectic enzyme		
Campden tablet		
Champagne wine yeast and nutrient		
Vitamin B_1	3mg	1 tablet
Sugar	70g	2½ oz
Champagne wine yeast		

PEARS

Pears were grown and cultivated in Britain long before the Romans came. It is believed that there are now between 900 and 1,000 different varieties, but only some ten or twelve are widely grown. Of these the most popular are Conference, William and Comice. The trees are not self-fertile and need to be grown not too far away from other varieties that will pollinate them. There are some culinary varieties especially suitable for winemaking but any variety, or mixture of varieties, will do provided that they are used as soon as they are picked and before they ripen fully. Soft pears do not make good wine.

Although pears contain almost as much sugar as eating apples they contain only half as much acid (mostly malic). Additional acid is therefore essential when making pear wine. A wide range of vitamins and mineral salts is present, but vitamin B_1 is on the low side and fermentation would benefit from the addition of a Benerva tablet. The flavour elements in pears are delicate rather than robust and there is some tannin in the skins. This makes them very suitable for blending with red fruits of strong flavour. The delicate flavour is also a reason why pears are particularly suitable for making into sparkling wine.

Cut off the stems, wash and crush the pears or cut them into thin slices, drop them at once into a bin containing the water, washed and chopped sultanas, the tartaric acid, pectic enzyme and one crushed Campden tablet. Cover and leave for 24 hours.

Stir in the activated wine yeast, nutrient and Benerva tablet, and ferment on the pulp for six days, keeping the pears submerged or gently pressed down twice each day.

Strain out, press dry and discard the pulp, stir in the sugar and pour the must into a demijohn. Top up if necessary, fit an airlock and ferment out.

Rack into a clean jar, seal and store in a cold place until the wine is bright, then rack again and store for a total of at least six months.

Remove some must, stir in the priming sugar and the second yeast, return this to the jar, fit an airlock and leave in a warm place for a few hours.

As soon as fermentation begins, rack into sterilised champagne bottles. Seal with hollow-domed plastic stoppers and wire cages. Lay the bottles on their sides and leave them in a warm room for one week and a cool store for six months.

Remove the sediment as described on pages 33 and 34.

PLUMS AND GAGES

Plums and gages were introduced into Britain from France and Italy about the middle of the fifteenth century. They rapidly established themselves as firm favourites for tarts, pies and jams and continued to enjoy great popularity for some 500 years. They were widely grown in Worcestershire and Kent, then known as the garden of England. Culinary plums were very cheap and, apart from making excellent jam for use all the year round, they were bottled by almost every housewife for winter use. In the countryside every kind of plum was used for making wines that kept well because of the high acidity of the fruit (mostly malic acid). Then suddenly, after the Second World War ended in 1945, the interest in plums waned. Possibly the shortage of sugar until 1952 and its increasing cost had something to do with it. Maybe the increasing affluence in the 1960s caused many people to look down on the common and humble plum. Whatever the reason, plums are now much more expensive than they used to be. Nevertheless, if you can find a good source of supply, do make some plum wine.

Victoria plums, the size and shape of a chicken's egg, and medium red-yellow in colour, make a superb sherry-style wine. The round black plums make a light red luncheon wine. The light red plum, like a bantam egg in shape and size, makes a fine rosé wine; the golden plums and greengages make excellent dry white wines, the golden having an affinity to Hock and the gage to Chablis.

Because of their popularity for jam, plums contain pectin and so a pectolytic enzyme must always be added to the must. Plums also have a peculiar waxy bloom that can come through to the finished wine. They should be soaked in hot water containing a little washing soda for about one minute, and then rinsed in running cold water. Finally, the stones must be removed and discarded. Failure to do so may cause an unpleasant taste in the wine, similar to bitter almonds. It is often a tedious task to remove the stones, but it is absolutely essential to do so. They can be removed most easily from fully ripe fruit, but do not use over-ripe, damaged or mouldy plums.

Greengage table wine

Greengages	2 kg	4½ lb
Sultanas	250g	9 oz
Sugar	800g	1¾ lb
Water	3.4 l	6 pt
Pectic enzyme		
Campden tablets		
Chablis wine yeast		

No acid needed.

Stalk, wash in hot water, stone and crush the fruit. Place in a bin with the washed and chopped sultanas, pour on the water, stir in the pectic enzyme and one crushed Campden tablet. Cover and leave for 24 hours.

Mix in the activated yeast and ferment on the pulp for four days, keeping the fruit submerged, or gently pressed down twice each day.

Strain out, press dry and discard the pulp, stir in the sugar, pour the must into a demijohn, fit an airlock and ferment to dryness in a cool temperature.

Rack into a storage jar, add one Campden tablet and mature for one year before bottling.

Serve this wine cold, with fish, pork or poultry.

Plum rosé wine

Early River plums	2 kg	4½ lb
Sultanas	250g	9 oz
Sugar	800g	1¾ lb
Hot water	3.4 l	6 pt
Tannin	2.5ml	½ tsp
Pectic enzyme		
Campden tablets		
Bordeaux wine yeast		

No acid needed.

Stalk, wash in hot water, stone and crush the

fruit, pour on hot water, cover and leave to cool, but stir from time to time to help the extraction of colour.

Mix in the washed and chopped sultanas, the pectic enzyme and one crushed Campden tablet. Cover and leave for 24 hours.

Mix in the activated wine yeast and tannin, and ferment on pulp for four days, keeping the fruit submerged or gently pressed down twice each day.

Strain out, press dry and discard the pulp, stir in the sugar, pour the must into a demijohn, fit an airlock and ferment to dryness in a cool temperature.

Rack into a storage jar, add one Campden tablet and mature for one year before bottling. Sweeten slightly with one saccharin tablet per bottle.

Serve this wine cold at picnics or parties, or with ham or snacks in the home.

Plum table wine

Blue/black plums	2 kg	4½ lb
Sultanas	250g	9 oz
Sugar	900g	2 lb
Hot water	3.4 l	6 pt
Tannin	5ml	1 tsp
Pectic enzyme		
Campden tablets		
Burgundy wine yeast		

No acid needed.

Stalk, wash in hot water, stone and crush the fruit, pour on hot water, cover and leave to cool, but stir from time to time to help the extraction of colour.

Mix in the washed and chopped sultanas, the pectic enzyme and one crushed Campden tablet. Cover and leave for 24 hours.

Mix in the activated wine yeast and tannin, and ferment on pulp for four days, keeping the fruit submerged or gently pressed down twice each day.

Strain out, press dry and discard the pulp, stir in the sugar, pour the must into a demijohn, fit an airlock and ferment to dryness in a cool temperature.

Rack into a storage jar, add one Campden tablet and mature for one year before bottling. Sweeten slightly with one saccharin tablet per bottle.

Serve free from chill with red meats and cheese. It is particularly suitable as a luncheon wine.

Plum aperitif

Victoria plums	2 kg	4½ lb
Sultanas	250g	9 oz
Sugar	1.125 kg	2½ lb
Cold water	3.4 l	6 pt
Vitamin B_1	3 mg	1 tablet
Pectic enzyme		
Campden tablet		
Fino Sherry yeast and nutrient		

No acid needed.

Stalk, wash in hot water, stone and crush the fruit, add the washed and chopped sultanas, then pour on the cold water. Stir in the pectic enzyme and one crushed Campden tablet, cover and leave in a warm place for 24 hours.

Stir in the activated yeast, crushed Vitamin B_1 tablet and nutrient. Ferment on the pulp for five days, keeping the fruit submerged or gently pressed down twice each day.

Strain out, press dry and discard the fruit, stir in half the sugar and continue fermentation in the bin covered with a thick cloth or in a demijohn plugged with cotton wool.

After ten days, stir in half the remaining sugar, and after another seven days, stir in the rest.

When fermentation finishes, check the specific gravity. If it is 0.996 or lower, stir in one level tablespoonful of sugar. If fermentation starts again, feed the must with one level tablespoonful of sugar every three or four days until fermentation finally stops. The final reading should not be higher than 1.000 unless a slightly sweeter finish is preferred.

Rack the wine from its sediment and mature for at least two years in a jar not quite full and plugged with cotton wool instead of a bung.

Serve chilled before meals.

Prune aperitif

Large prunes	1 kg	2¼ lb
Rosehips	250g	9 oz
Sultanas	250g	9 oz
Sugar	1.35 kg	3 lb
Citric acid	10 ml	2 tsp
Water	3.7 l	6½ pt
Vitamin B$_1$	3 mg	1 tablet

Pectic enzyme
Campden tablet
Sherry yeast and nutrient

Wash the prunes in warm water, drain and place them in a large bowl. Top and tail the rosehips, crush them open and add to the prunes. Pour on hot water, cover and leave overnight.

Bring to the boil, simmer for 20 minutes, then leave to cool. Remove and discard the prune stones, crush the pulp with a potato masher, add the acid, pectic enzyme and one crushed Campden tablet. Cover and leave for 24 hours.

Strain out, press dry and discard the pulp, add the washed and chopped sultanas, the Vitamin B$_1$ tablet, the nutrient and activated yeast. Ferment in a covered bin or in a demijohn plugged with cotton wool, making sure that the sultanas are kept moist for five days.

Strain out, press dry and discard the sultanas, stir in one-third of the sugar and continue fermentation.

One week later, stir in half the remaining sugar and one week later, stir in the rest.

At the end of fermentation, rack into a storage vessel and check the specific gravity. If the reading is below 1.016 stir in sufficient sugar to increase the reading to this figure.

Mature this wine for two years in a vessel plugged with cotton wool instead of a bung.

Serve this wine cold for those who like a sweeter aperitif.

QUINCE

There are two kinds of quince that can be used by the winemaker. The best one to use is the European *Pyrus cydonia*. The fruit is produced on a tree that lives to a great age. The flowers are a waxy white or pink. The fruit can be either apple or pear-shaped and is a brilliant golden-yellow. It is harvested in October when still very hard and should be left to mellow for five or six weeks.

Even so, the fruit is too hard and too sour to be eaten raw and is best made into wine or jelly. It has a delicious and very strong aroma and for this reason makes a splendid additive to apple wine.

The second kind is the ornamental shrub, *Cydonia japonica*. There are a number of different varieties, some with waxy white flowers, some with pink and some with a glorious scarlet red that appears in January before the leaves. The flavour of the fruit depends on the variety and the author prefers the small, yellow, bantam-egg size. Other varieties of this shrub produce larger fruit with less aroma. Like the European variety, the japonica fruit is hard and very acid. Quince makes very good jelly and it is high in pectin; an extra dose of pectolytic enzyme should be added to the must, therefore, to break down the pectin.

The skin is high in phenolics (bitter substances), but these reduce during the mellowing period. The pulp contains a large quantity of malic acid that also reduces during mellowing. Conversely the sugar content increases and can reach as much as 10%. Vitamin C is present in the form of ascorbic acid.

Quince sweet wine

Mellow quince	3 kg	6¾ lb
Sultanas	250g	9 oz
Sugar	1.5 kg	3½ lb
Citric acid	15 ml	3 tsp
Water	3 l	5¼ pt

Campden tablets
Pectic enzyme
Tokay wine yeast and nutrient

Wash and crush the quince and if possible exclude the great number of black pips. Drop the fruit into a bin containing the washed and chopped sultanas, the citric acid, pectic enzyme and one crushed Campden tablet. Cover and leave for 24 hours.

Stir in the activated yeast and nutrient and ferment on the pulp for five days, keeping the fruit submerged or gently pressed down twice each day.

Strain out, press dry and discard the pulp, stir in one-third of the sugar, pour the must into a demijohn, fit an airlock and ferment for one week.

Remove some must, stir in half the remaining sugar, return this to the jar and continue the fermentation.

One week later repeat the process with the last of the sugar and ferment to a finish.

Rack into a storage jar and keep for at least one year before bottling.

Serve this strong sweet wine after meals.

RASPBERRY

Since the advent of home freezers, this delicious summer fruit is now available the whole year round. It enables us to blend down its high acidity and pronounced flavour with other ingredients to make very attractive pretty pink wines for parties and picnics. By itself its flavour is too strong for a table wine, but it can be made into a dessert wine of great character after several years in store. No additional acid would be needed in the must.

Surprisingly, raspberries are not very sweet and 500g (18 oz) of fruit only contribute about 30g (1 oz) of sugar to a gallon of must.

A number of different varieties are available but those developed by the Malling Horticultural Research Institute are among the best. In order of fruiting, they are Malling Promise, Malling Jewel and Malling Admiral. Other popular varieties include Norfolk Giant, Hailsham and September. There is no evidence as to the one most suitable for making wine. The tendency is to reserve the largest berries for eating fresh or frozen and to use the smaller berries and any that get damaged in the picking for making wine!

Raspberries, like blackberries, should be picked quite dry and preferably in sunshine. Remove stalks and shreds of leaf, grade them, if necessary, and use them, or freeze them as quickly as possible.

Raspberry dessert wine

Raspberries	1.8 kg	4 lb
*Concentrated grape juice	250g	9 oz
Sugar	1.35 kg	3 lb
*Tannin	2.5 ml	½ tsp
Water	3.4 l	6 pt
Campden tablet		
Pectic enzyme		
Tokay wine yeast and nutrient		

*The concentrated grape juice may be red or white. Use 5 ml/1 tsp tannin with the red and 2.5 ml/½ tsp with the white. Alternatively sultanas may be used but these are less suitable in this recipe than the grape juice.

Stalk, wash and liquidise the raspberries, add the concentrated grape juice, pectic enzyme and one crushed Campden tablet, then dilute with cold water. Cover and leave for 24 hours in a warm place (24–25°C/75–77°F).

Strain through a fine meshed nylon sieve, shake gently and discard the fairly dry pulp.

Mix in the tannin and the activated wine yeast, and nutrient, pour the must into a demijohn, fit an airlock and ferment for 4 days.

Remove some wine, stir in one-third of the

sugar, return this to the jar and ferment for a week.

Repeat this process with half the remaining sugar and one week later with the rest.

When fermentation is finished, rack into a storage jar and mature for two years.

Serve after meals as a sweet and strong wine.

NOTE

A small quantity of raspberries improves the flavour of other red wines.

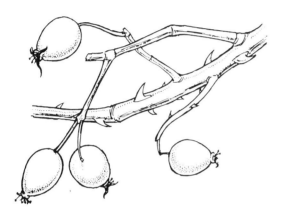

ROSE HIPS

Our ancestors knew that rose hips were beneficial to health and used them to make jams, jellies, syrups and sauces as well as tart fillings. It was not until the 1930s, however, that the special health-promoting properties of rose hips were discovered. The fruit is exceptionally rich in vitamin C (20 times more than oranges – weight for weight), and also contains vitamins A, B, E and P.

The rose hip to use is from the dog rose (*Rosa canina*) that grows wild in the hedgerows. In the summer its pale pink, heart-shaped petals surrounding a crown of golden stamens may be used to make a very delicate wine. In the autumn its orange-scarlet elongated berries, often growing in clusters of three, may be not only picked to make a rose hip wine, but also used as an additive to many other wines to give body and nourishment. Cut off the stalks and black flower seat then wash the berries in a weak sulphite solution. They may be used at once, or drained, packed into polythene bags and frozen for future use.

Rose hip wine

Rose hips	3.4 l	6 pt
Sultanas	250g	9 oz
Lemons	2	
Sugar	1 kg	2¼ lb
Water	4 l	7 pt
Pectic enzyme		
Campden tablets		
Sauternes wine yeast and nutrient		

Top and tail the ripe berries, wash them and crush them without breaking the inner pips. Thinly pare and chop the yellow lemon skins (no white pith). Wash and chop the sultanas. Place them all in a bin and pour boiling water over them. Cover and leave to cool.

Express and strain the lemon juice and add this to the bin with the pectic enzyme and one crushed Campden tablet. Cover and leave for 24 hours.

Add the nutrient and activated yeast and ferment for five days keeping the pulp submerged or gently pressed down twice each day.

Strain out, press dry and discard the pulp; stir in the sugar; pour the must into a demijohn, fit an airlock and ferment to a finish.

Rack into a storage jar, add one Campden tablet, seal and store for one year or more before bottling.

Serve cold, sweetened to taste if necessary, with sweet biscuits.

ROWANBERRY

Although a member of the rose family, the rowan tree (*Sorbus aucuparia*) grows to a height of nine metres (30 feet) or more, on a straight, clean and narrow trunk. Its popular name is mountain ash, but it grows in thickets and hedgerows as well as in woods and rocky glens. It is also widely cultivated.

Long before the Christian faith was preached in Britain and for long afterwards, too, the rowan was revered as a defence against attacks by witches and demons. A bunch of rowan twigs bound with a piece of red thread or braid would be hung at the lintel to keep out all unwanted and evil spirits. In the autumn, cows in calf would be fed bunches of berries to ensure a trouble-free confinement.

Colour has long played a great part in the beliefs of mankind. As recently as the sixteenth and seventeenth centuries physicians believed that red wine, because it was the colour of fire, heated the alimentary system and caused particles to synthesise into stones that collected in the kidneys and bladder. Conversely, white wine, because it was the colour of water, was thought to cool the system and wash away impurities and unwanted elements. It is reasonable to assume that the rowan was much favoured because of the countless generous bunches of shining orange-scarlet berries hanging from the bright green foliage. Because they looked so good, it was thought that they must be good. Birds still agree, for the berries are an important source of food in their winter foraging.

To the human palate freshly picked rowanberries taste sharp and bitter, but when used to make a jelly to serve with cold meats they are said to be delicious.

I have not been very successful in using rowanberries to make wine. Even at 1 kg per 5 litres (2 lb per gallon), the wine was extremely bitter. The berries contain a substance called amygdalin which is a source of small quantities of hydrogen cyanide – a powerful poison in a large enough dose. But 2 lbs of rowanberries in a gallon of wine produce no more than one-third of a lethal dose. More to the point, you would have to drink the whole gallon in one go to absorb the third! There is not really much danger from poisoning, then. The bitter flavour remains the enemy.

If you are especially keen to use rowan-berries, it is suggested that you use no more than 250g per 5 litres (9 oz to the gallon), mixed with other fruits to make an aperitif-type wine. With so many other good fruits readily available, I feel that rowanberries just aren't worth the trouble.

RHUBARB

Our culinary rhubarb is not a native of the United Kingdom. Although it is nearly always used as a fruit, it is, strictly speaking, a vegetable. The leaves contain a substantial quantity of oxalic acid necessary for the metabolism of the plant, but this is largely neutralised before it enters the stalk. It follows, then, that whilst the leaf is poisonous, the stalk is quite safe to eat. the fairly high acid content of the stalks is due almost entirely to malic acid and the oxalic acid present is less than 5% of the total acid – not as much as in bananas. The stalk does contain a tiny quantity of calcium oxalate, however, that increases with age. Late-gathered rhubarb is not recommended for wine, any more than forced rhubarb. The best rhubarb is harvested in May and June, depending on the earliness or lateness of the season.

Some winemakers hold the view that calcium carbonate (common chalk) should be added to the must to remove the small quantity of oxalic acid and the oxalates. This is quite unnecessary and, indeed, deleterious for it diminishes the unique flavour of rhubarb. It also removes the malic acid which must be replaced with citric or tartaric acid. In my view, de-acidification of the must is both unnecessary and undesirable.

The Champagne variety of rhubarb with its bright red stalks is the most suitable variety to use for making wine, especially if no other basic ingredient is to be used. The resulting wine has a delicate pink hue and the flavour is light and subtle, rather than pronounced.

Rhubarb blends very well with other ingredients, especially those lacking acid

67

Country fruits and their wines

such as dates, figs, prunes, marrow, melon, cereals, flowers and vegetables.

When preparing rhubarb stalks, cut off the white foot and about 2.5 cm (1 inch) below the leaf. Wipe the stalks with a clean cloth that has been freshly soaked in a sulphite solution, then liquidise them, mince them in a stainless steel mincer, or chop them up as finely as you can.

Rhubarb wine

Rhubarb	2 kg	4½ lb
Sultanas	250g	9 oz
Bananas	250g	9 oz
Sugar	1 kg	2¼ lb
Water	3.4 l	6 pt
Pectic enzyme		
Campden tablets		
Sauternes wine yeast and nutrient		

No acid needed.

Top and tail the rhubarb, wipe the stalks with a cloth soaked in a sulphite solution, then chop up the stalks, mince or liquidise them, together with the washed sultanas and peeled bananas.

Pour on cold water, stir in the pectic enzyme and one crushed Campden tablet. Cover and leave for 24 hours.

Mix in the activated wine yeast and nutrient, and ferment for four days keeping the fruit submerged, or gently pressed down twice each day.

Strain out, press dry and discard the pulp, stir in the sugar, pour the must into a demijohn, fit an airlock and ferment out.

Rack into a storage jar, add one Campden tablet, seal and keep for one year before bottling. Sweeten to taste with saccharin if necessary.

Serve cold with biscuits.

SLOE

The blackthorn (*Prunus spinosa*) is another of our many hedgerow shrubs. In the early spring its pure white, starry flowers on bare black branches foretell the coming of warmer

weather. In the autumn its Prussian-blue berries, like tiny plums, provide us with a bitter-sharp fruit, ideal for making wine and sloe gin. The berries tend to grow singly on branches well protected with long sharp thorns. They are best gathered in November, after an early frost has diminished the acid and increased the sugar content. Because of the thorns it is advisable to wear leather gloves when picking sloes.

The berries are covered with a bloom and contain a single stone. It is neither possible, nor necessary, to remove the stone when using the berries for wine or liqueur.

The colour is in the skin and, as with other members of the plum family, is not easy to remove. It is necessary first to pour hot water over the berries and when cool to ferment them on the pulp for a few days to leach out as much colour as you can. The resulting red is not nearly so dark as you would expect from the blue-black skin.

A table wine can be made from sloes but their strong flavour and high acid and tannin content make a better dessert wine.

Sloe dessert wine

Sloes	2.25 kg	5 lb
Sultanas	250g	9 oz
Sugar	1.35 kg	3 lb
Citric acid	10 ml	2 tsp
Tannin	5 ml	1 tsp
Water	3.7 l	6½ pt

Pectic enzyme
Campden tablet
Port wine yeast and nutrient

Stalk, and wash the sloes, pour boiling water over them, cover and leave to cool.

Add the washed and chopped sultanas, the acid, pectic enzyme and one crushed Campden tablet. Cover and leave for 24 hours.

Mix in the tannin, activated yeast and nutrient and ferment for four days, keeping the fruit submerged to obtain good colour extraction.

Strain out, press dry and discard the pulp, stir in one-third of the sugar, pour the must into a demijohn, fit an airlock and ferment for one week.

Remove some must, stir in half the remaining sugar, return this to the jar and continue fermentation.

One week later, repeat this process with the last of the sugar and ferment to a finish.

Rack into a storage jar, seal and keep for two years.

Serve this strong sweet wine after meals.

SUMMER FRUIT WINE

The soft fruits of summer always seem to be in short supply. We never seem to have a surplus and it is difficult to spare enough to make wine from any one fruit. Quite often, however, a few can be spared from the many different kinds that one grows; furthermore, many of the fruits are so strongly flavoured and high in acid that it makes good sense to blend together as many different kinds as you can, bearing in mind their different contents and making sure that you balance the must in respect of acid, sugar, tannin and flavour. Make your selection from the following:

Black, red and white currants
strawberries
early blackberries
plums
imported seedless grapes
a few ripe bananas
cherries
gooseberries
raspberries
early eating apples
loganberries
peaches
melon.
Whatever is about.

Be careful not to use more than 200g (7 oz) each of blackcurrants, raspberries and loganberries in particular, but make a total fruit content up to at least 1.5 kg (3½ lb). A suggested recipe follows but it can be varied to suit the fruits that you have available. This recipe is for a party wine not too high in alcohol (about 12%) and finished with just enough sweetness to mask the slightly high acidity and to balance the splendid flavour.

Summer fruit wine

Blackberries	250g	9 oz
Blackcurrants	200g	7 oz
Eating apples	450g	1 lb
Gooseberries	200g	7 oz
Raspberries	200g	7 oz
Redcurrants	200g	7 oz
Seedless grapes	450g	1 lb
Strawberries	200g	7 oz
Sugar	700g	1 lb 9 oz
Water	3.4 l	6 pt

Pectic enzyme
Campden tablets
Bordeaux wine yeast
Sweetening
No acid, tannin or nutrient required.

Clean, wash and crush the fruit and cover it with cold water, stir in the pectic enzyme and one crushed Campden tablet. Cover and leave for 24 hours.

Stir in an activated wine yeast and ferment on the pulp for four days, keeping the fruit submerged or gently pressed down twice each day.

Strain out, press dry and discard the fruit, stir in the sugar, pour the must into a demijohn, fit an airlock and continue fermentation to the end.

Rack into a storage jar, add one Campden tablet, seal and keep in a cold place until the wine is bright, then rack again and keep for one year.

Take the edge off the dryness of this wine with one saccharin pellet per bottle before serving, and serve it cold at picnics or parties, with cold meat and salads and with snacks.

7 Root vegetables

When serving root vegetables we often throw away many beneficial elements with the water in which they were cooked. Winemakers have long known this and use this liquor for making wine.

Beetroot, carrots and parsnips can all be used to make wine, whilst at the same time providing vegetables to eat. Mangold, sugar beet and turnip, however, are not worth the effort involved.

Select mature vegetables from the main crop as soon as they are ready. If possible dig them freshly for the purpose and use them at once. Scrub them clean in plenty of cold water, remove the tail and the crown and cut them into thin rings or small dice-sized pieces. Boil them in the recommended quantity of water until the pieces are soft and tender but not mushy.

Root vegetables make better dessert wines than table wines, but when combined with figs, parsnips also make an interesting aperitif-style wine.

Beetroot dessert wine

Beetroot	2 kg	4½ lb
Raisins	500g	18 oz
Sugar	1 kg	2¼ lb
Water	4 l	7 pt
Citric acid	15 ml	3 tsp
Grape tannin	5 ml	1 tsp
Port wine yeast and nutrient		

Strain the hot beetroot liquor onto the washed and chopped raisins, cover and leave to cool. Mix in the acid, tannin and the activated wine yeast.

Ferment on the pulp for seven days, keeping the raisins submerged or gently pressed down twice each day.

Strain out, press dry and discard the raisins, stir in one-third of the sugar, pour the must into a fermentation jar, leaving room for the rest of the sugar.

After seven days, remove some must, stir in half the remaining sugar, return to the jar and continue the fermentation.

Seven days later repeat this process with the rest of the sugar and ferment to a finish.

Rack into a clean jar, check the specific gravity and, if necessary, stir in sufficient sugar to raise the reading to 1.020. Seal and store the wine until it is bright, then rack again and mature this strong wine for two years in bulk before bottling.

Keep it for a further six months, or longer, then serve it after the evening meal.

Root vegetables

Carrot dessert wine

Carrots	2 kg	4½ lb
Sultanas	500g	18 oz
Sugar	1 kg	2¼ lb
Water	4 l	7 pt
Citric acid	15 ml	3 tsp
Grape tannin	2.5 ml	½ tsp

Tokay wine yeast and nutrient

Make in exactly the same way as described for beetroot wine.

Parsnip sherry

Parsnip	2 kg	4½ lb
Dried figs	200g	7 oz
Sultanas	500g	18 oz
Sugar	1 kg	2¼ lb
Citric acid	15 ml	3 tsp
Grape tannin	5 ml	1 tsp
Water	4 l	7 pt

Sherry wine yeast and nutrient

Strain the hot parsnip liquor onto the broken up figs, and the washed and chopped sultanas, cover and leave to cool.

Mix in the acid, tannin and the activated yeast. Ferment on the pulp for seven days, keeping the fruit submerged, or gently pressed down twice each day.

Strain out, press dry and discard the pulp, stir in one-third of the sugar and continue fermentation in the bin covered with a thick cloth.

After seven days, stir in half the remaining sugar and one week later mix in the rest. Continue the fermentation in the bin or in a jar plugged with cotton wool.

When fermentation has finished and the wine begins to clear, rack into a jar leaving an airspace above the wine and plug the neck of the jar with cotton wool.

Store for two years like this, then bottle. The sherry-like flavour can be enhanced by mixing the wine with one bottle of Spanish sherry when the wine is bright and being racked.

NOTE
Made without figs and a Tokay yeast instead of a sherry yeast, the parsnip liquor can be made into a strong and sweet dessert wine in the same way as described for beetroot wine.

POTATO

Some people believe that the potato was introduced into Britain by Sir Walter Raleigh. Others believe that Sir Francis Drake was more likely to have brought it home from his raids on South America in 1586. For 150 years the potato was used primarily for cattle food, then came the Irish and Scottish famines of the eighteenth century and its value as an important food for humans was realised. The potato contains less sugar and more starch than any other root vegetable and is very rich in magnesium, phosphorus and potassium, as well as Vitamin B_1. It also contains more protein than other root vegetables.

When using potatoes for winemaking always include some fungal amylase to convert the starch into sugar so that the yeast enzymes can convert the sugar into alcohol.

The following recipe is my favourite for potatoes, but it does take a long time to mature. However, the result is well worth the wait.

Potato dessert wine

Small old potatoes	1 kg	2¼ lb
Raisins	500g	18 oz
Pearl barley	250g	9 oz
Fresh lemons	2	
Seville oranges	2	
Demerara sugar	1.35 kg	3 lb
Fungal amylase	quantity on packet	
Water	4 l	7 pt

Tokay or Madeira wine yeast and nutrient

Scrub the potatoes clean and grate them or cut them into thin slices. Place them in a

72

polythene bin together with the washed and chopped raisins and crushed pearl barley. Add the thinly pared rind of the lemons and the oranges and pour boiling water over them.

Stir well and when the temperature reaches 75°C (167°F), mix in the fungal amylase, cover the vessel and leave to cool.

Stir in the expressed and strained juice from the lemons and oranges, the nutrient and an activated Tokay or Madeira wine yeast to ensure a high alcohol wine.

Ferment on the pulp for one week, then strain out and press the solids dry; stir in one-third of the sugar, pour the must into a demijohn, leaving room for the rest of the sugar. Fit an airlock and ferment for one week.

Remove some must, stir in half the remaining sugar, return this to the jar and continue the fermentation.

One week later add the rest of the sugar and continue fermentation to the end.

Rack into a storage jar, seal, label and mature for at least two years in bulk. Bottle and keep for a further year.

Serve this strong, sweet golden wine after the evening meal.

Potato social wine

Small old potatoes	2 kg	4½ lbs
Water	4 l	7 pt
Raisins	250g	9 oz
Lemons	3	
Fresh ginger root	1 large piece	
Sugar	1.35 kg	3 lb
Cereal wine yeast and nutrient		

Scrub the potatoes, cut them up into small pieces and boil them until tender but not mushy.

Strain into a bin containing the washed and chopped raisins, the thinly pared rinds of the lemons and the grated fresh ginger root. Cover and leave to cool.

Stir in the expressed and strained lemon juice, the nutrient and the activated cereal wine yeast (this yeast is also able to ferment the dissolved starch in the potato liquor). Ferment for three days, keeping the raisins submerged.

Strain out, press dry and discard the raisins. Stir in one-third of the sugar and continue as directed for the sweet wine recipe.

This wine matures just a little before the wine from the other recipe, but do keep it for as long as you can.

8 Surface vegetables

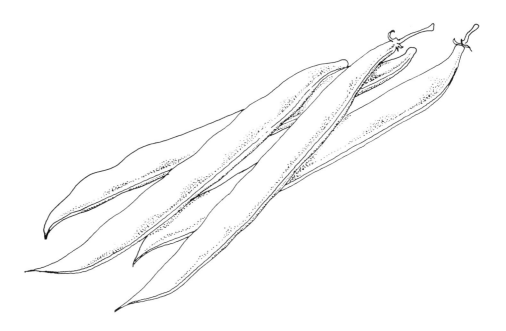

BEANS

Although not the best ingredient for making wine, beans have been used successfully on many occasions. There are never enough to spare of the tender French beans, but the broad beans and runner beans can often be used. Unless the blackfly has decimated your broad beans, it is likely that at the end of the season there will be a fair number of tough pods left hanging on the plants. These are just what is wanted. Shell the beans and discard the pods. Boil the beans until they are soft, but not mushy, and use the liquor for making the wine.

Pour the hot bean liquor onto the washed and chopped sultanas and the thinly pared and chopped rind of the lemon. Cover and leave to cool.

Stir in the malic acid, the expressed and strained juice of the lemon, the nutrient and an active wine yeast. Ferment for four days, keeping the sultanas submerged or gently pressed down twice a day.

Strain out, press dry and discard the sultanas, stir in the sugar, pour the must into a demijohn, fit an airlock and ferment to a finish.

Rack into a storage jar, add the Campden tablet, seal and store for nine months, then bottle. If necessary, sweeten to taste with saccharin and serve this light wine chilled.

Broad bean table wine

Broad beans	1.5 kg	3½ lb
Sultanas	250g	9 oz
Lemon	1	
Malic acid	10 ml	2 tsp
Sugar	900g	2 lb
Water	4 l	7 pt
Hock wine yeast and nutrient		
Campden tablet		

74

Runner bean table wine

Runner beans are nearly always trimmed lengthwise before being cooked. These trimmings can be used to make a wine by itself (a bit lacking in flavour) or added to an elderberry must to increase the body of that wine. A fair number of trimmings are needed. These could be taken in the middle of the season when the crop is heaviest and the beans are being processed for freezing.

Runner bean trimmings	1 kg	2¼ lb
Cleaned elderberries	1 kg	2¼ lb
Sultanas	250g	9 oz
Citric acid	15 ml	3 tsp
Sugar	1 kg	2¼ lb
Water	4 l	7 pt

Burgundy wine yeast and nutrient

Wash and chop up the bean trimmings, then place them in an aluminium or stainless steel preserving pan, together with the washed and crushed elderberries. Bring to the boil and simmer for 20 minutes. Keep the pan covered if possible, during both the simmering and subsequent cooling.

Strain through a nylon bag, press dry and discard the pulp, mix in the washed and chopped sultanas, the citric acid, nutrient and an activated wine yeast. Ferment on the pulp for four days then strain out, press dry and discard the sultanas.

Stir in half the sugar, pour the must into a demijohn, fit an airlock and ferment for one week. Remove some must, stir in the rest of the sugar, return this to the jar and ferment to a finish.

Rack into a storage vessel, seal and keep for at least one year in bulk, preferably two, then bottle and keep for a further six months.

Serve free from chill with minced beef and pasta dishes, or with cheese.

Pea pod table wine

This wine is interesting because it makes a vinhos verdes-style wine. Select fresh, green, fleshy pods that have been freshly picked and shucked. The pods soon begin to deteriorate if left. Chop them up and boil them until soft and tender, then use only the liquor.

Pea pod table wine

Pea pods	2 kg	4½ lb
Sultanas	250g	9 oz
Sugar	800g	1¾ lb
Citric acid	15 ml	3 tsp
Water	4 l	7 pt

Hock wine yeast and nutrient

Pour the pea pod liquor over the washed and chopped sultanas, then cover and leave to cool.

Mix in the acid, nutrient and an active wine yeast and ferment on the pulp for four days, keeping the sultanas submerged, or at least pressed down twice each day.

Strain out, press dry and discard the fruit, stir in the sugar, pour the must into a demijohn, fit an airlock and ferment to dryness.

Rack into a storage jar, seal and store for six months. Siphon into bottles and add just a pinch of sugar (no more) to each bottle. The intention is to produce just a few bubbles, not a sparkling wine. Cork the bottles and store them in a warm room for a few days, then in a cool store for three months. Chill the wine before serving with grilled fish or even fish fingers.

CELERY

None of the salads makes an acceptable wine except celery. There is no extractable colour in tomato skins and no flavour either. Lettuce, cucumber and radish have been tried and hurriedly forgotten! Spinach has been tried but the flavour is rather bitter. The odour of the brassicas is totally off-putting in a wine and onions are also a disaster. Learn from the experiments of others and don't waste your time on these ingredients.

The celery plant grows wild in parts of Europe and has long been known to mankind. The ancient Greeks used to cultivate it for the medicinal value of its seeds. Wine made from celery was once thought to be particularly beneficial to people suffering from rheumatism. It is a light and pleasant wine worth making if you have grown more celery heads than you can consume.

Select fine specimens, cut off the root and all the green and golden leaves. Also remove the outer stalks if they are at all bruised or marked in any way; they can go into the stock pot for soup. Cut off the other stalks and chop them up into small dice-sized pieces. Place them in a pan with the water, bring to the boil and simmer them for 20 minutes or so until they are soft and tender. Strain out the solids and use the liquor for the wine.

Celery table wine

Celery pieces	2 kg	4½ lb
Sultanas	250g	9 oz
Citric acid	15 ml	3 tsp
Sugar	900g	2 lb
Water	4 l	7 pt

Hock wine yeast and nutrient
Campden tablet

Add the washed and chopped sultanas to the hot celery liquor, cover and leave to cool.

Stir in the acid, nutrient and the active wine yeast and ferment on the pulp for three days, keeping the sultanas submerged or well pressed down.

Strain out, press dry and discard the sultanas, stir in the sugar, pour the must into a demijohn, fit an airlock and ferment out.

Rack into a storage jar, add one Campden tablet, seal and keep for six months, then bottle and sweeten to taste with saccharin. One tablet per bottle should be enough.

Serve this wine cold with vegetarian dishes.

NOTE

In all of these recipes you could use 250g (9 oz) of concentrated white grape juice instead of the sultanas. Allow the liquor to cool, then mix in the concentrate, acid and yeast, pour the must into a demijohn, fit an airlock and ferment for 3 days. Then remove some must, stir in the sugar, return this to the jar and continue fermentation. Alternatively, a bottle of pure grape juice may be used. The small quantity of grape certainly improves the wines and is well worth the little extra cost per bottle.

MARROW, MELON AND PUMPKIN WINES

These three basic ingredients are not only somewhat similar in shape and texture, but also they all lack flavour in the finished wine. It is necessary to add some ginger, cloves, cinnamon, lemon skin, or a mixture of any or all of these spices to give the wines made from marrow, melon or pumpkin a bit of character. How much you add is a matter of personal taste. The flavouring needs to be subtle rather than pronounced. One large piece of fresh ginger root, grated, and, say, a dozen crushed cloves, a large stick of cinnamon crushed, the thinly pared skin of a large fresh lemon, or an orange, should be enough.

Honey could also be used but not more than, say, 250g (9 oz), preferably of a strong-flavoured variety, in one gallon of must. Another flavouring could be used, if you wished, in the form of scented rose petals or elderflowers. Whatever you use, don't forget to include the sultanas as well, for these form the real base of the wine.

Marrow, melon or		
pumpkin	2.5 kg	5½ lb
Sultanas	250g	9 oz
Flavouring	see above	
Sugar	1 kg	2¼ lb
Citric acid	15 ml	3 tsp
Water	2.8 l	5 pt
Hock wine yeast and nutrient		
Campden tablet		

Wipe over the surface of the marrow, melon or pumpkin with a cloth that has been soaked in a sulphite solution, then cut up into thin slices or small dice-sized pieces. Include the skin and pips but do not cut or break them.

Add the flavouring of your choice, the washed and chopped sultanas, the acid, nutrient and the activated yeast. Ferment on the pulp for three days, keeping the ingredients submerged, or gently pressed down twice each day.

Strain out, press dry and discard the pulp, stir in the sugar, pour the must into a demijohn, top up with cold water, if necessary, fit an airlock and ferment to a finish.

Rack into a storage jar, add one Campden tablet, seal and store for six months then bottle. The wine may have some residual sugar and taste sweetish; if not, sweeten it to taste with saccharin.

Serve it cold as a social wine and with a sweet biscuit or cake.

NOTE

Courgettes or miniature marrows may be used instead of the large marrow.

9 Flowers, follies, herbs and saps

FLOWERS

A walk along country lanes at different times of the year reveals many tempting flowers to make into wine. Some must be left alone, notably the cowslip which is a protected flower, while others like the snowdrop, crocus and bluebell are poisonous. Flowers contribute perfume to the bouquet and flavour of a wine but nothing else. They make an attractive social wine that stimulates conversation. It is important to serve them semi-sweet rather than dry or fully sweet. The sweet-smelling bouquet is contradicted by a dry taste, yet becomes cloying if the wine is too sweet. It is best to make them dry and to sweeten them to your taste when bottling with a non-fermentable wine sweetening.

When gathering flowers, always use baskets or paper bags, not plastic bags since these cause sweating. Pick them after the dew has dried but while they are fully open in the warmth of the mid-day sun. Remove every trace of stem, leaf and calyx and use only the petals. The green parts contain chlorophyl and impart a bitter taste to the wine.

Flowers that may be used are:

Yellow Broom: 4 pints of petals per gallon of wine
Carnations: 4 pints white petals per gallon of wine (garden pinks)
Clover: 4 pints purple petals per gallon of wine
Coltsfoot: 4 pints yellow petals per gallon of wine
Dandelion: 4 pints yellow petals per gallon of wine

Elderflowers: 1 pint cream florets per gallon of wine

Golden Rod: 1 pint golden florets per gallon of wine

Lime: 4 pints bracts with flowers per gallon of wine

Primrose: 4 pints yellow petals per gallon of wine

Rose: 4 pints scented petals per gallon of wine

The flower water is always prepared in the same way. Place the petals in a ceramic bowl and pour boiling water on them. Rub the flowers against the side of the bowl with the back of a wooden spoon to extract the flavouring essences. Do this several times a day to extract as much flavour as possible. When the water cools, add one crushed Campden tablet and one level teaspoonful of citric acid. Continue macerating for three days, then strain out, press dry and discard the petals. Use this liquor for making the wine.

Flower water wines

Flower water	3.4 l	6 pt
Sultanas	500g	18 oz
Sugar	680g	1½ lb
Citric acid	10 ml	2 tsp
All-purpose wine yeast and nutrient		
Campden tablet		
Sweetening		

Add the washed and chopped sultanas to the flower water, stir in the acid, nutrient and an activated wine yeast. Cover and ferment on the pulp for seven days, keeping the sultanas submerged, or gently pressed down twice daily.

Strain out, press dry and discard the sultanas, stir in the sugar, pour the must into a demijohn, fit an airlock and ferment to a finish.

Rack into a clean jar, add one Campden tablet, seal and store for six months. Bottle and sweeten to taste.

Serve these wines chilled with sweet biscuits.

FOLLIES

The word folly usually describes an act of foolishness – the opposite of wise. In the context of winemaking, however, folly has an entirely different meaning. It is derived from the French word *feuille*, meaning leaf'. Accordingly, wines made from suitable leaves are often called follies, but are far from foolish.

The most popular follies are made from the summer prunings of grape vines (see page 00), and brambles, but walnut leaves, oak leaves and tea leaves can also be used. Like petals, leaves contribute little more than flavour and always need to be supported by sultanas, acid and nutrient.

Vine and bramble prunings should be taken before a fungicide spray, but even so, they need to be well washed in cold water before use. The leaves/prunings must then be chopped up into small lengths, simmered in the water for 15 minutes at 80°C (176°F), left to cool, strained, and the liquor used for making one gallon of wine. Alternatively, the chopped pieces may be packed into one-pound polythene bags and frozen until required. You can use one pound of vine prunings as an additive to enhance the flavour and body of a gallon of another wine.

Bramble folly table wine

Bramble prunings	3 kg	6¾ lb
Concentrated grape juice	500g	18 oz
Sugar	680g	1½ lb
Citric acid	10 ml	2 tsp
Water	3.4 l	6 pt
Hock wine yeast and nutrient		
Campden tablet		

Mix the concentrated grape juice into the cool folly liquor, stir in the acid, nutrient and the activated yeast, pour the must into a demijohn, fit an airlock and ferment for seven days.

Remove some of the must, stir in the sugar and, when it is dissolved, return it to the jar. Continue fermentation to the end.

Rack into a clean jar, add one Campden

tablet, seal and store for six months. Bottle and sweeten to taste with saccharin (one or two pellets per bottle).

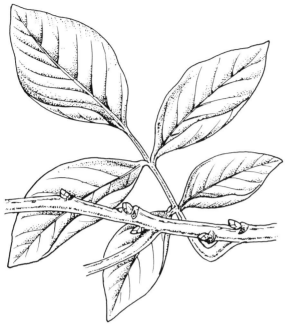

Walnut leaves bestow a pleasant nutty flavour to a wine and a few added to a sherry-style wine are advantageous. Oak leaves contain a good deal of tannin, and a few added to many of our red wines could be beneficial – say, a small handful per gallon. Both oak and walnut leaves are best picked young – as soon as they are full size and full of sap. Pick only the best looking leaves and avoid those with blemishes of any kind. They should all be washed before use. One pint of leaves is sufficient to flavour one gallon of wine.

Leaf table wine

Oak or walnut leaves	560 ml	1 pt
Concentrated grape juice	500g	18 oz
Sugar	680g	1½ lb
Citric acid	10 ml	2 tsp
Water	3.4 l	6 pt

All-purpose wine yeast and nutrient
Campden tablets

Chop up the leaves and simmer them in the water for 15 minutes at 80°C (176°F) in a covered pan. Strain through a nylon bag into a bin, cover and leave to cool. Discard the leaves. Stir in the grape juice, acid and an activated wine yeast. Pour the must into a demijohn, fit an airlock and ferment for seven days.

Take out some must, stir in the sugar and return it to the jar. Continue fermentation to the end.

Rack into a storage jar, add one Campden tablet, seal and keep for six months. Bottle and sweeten to taste with saccharin.

Tea wine

Tea leaves are best used to make a fresh brew and the liquor used for the wine. The tea of your choice may be used and each tea variety will make a different wine. One that is not too strong, nor too highly scented might be preferred.

Tea wine

Tea bags	12	
Sultanas	500g	18 oz
Sugar	680g	1½ lb
Citric acid	10 ml	2 tsp
Water	4 l	7 pt

All-purpose wine yeast and nutrient
Campden tablet

Pour boiling water on the tea bags and leave for five minutes. Remove and press the tea bags, add the washed and chopped sultanas and leave to cool.

Stir in the citric acid and an activated yeast. Ferment on the pulp for seven days, keeping the sultanas submerged or gently pressed down twice each day.

Strain out, press dry and discard the sultanas, stir in the sugar and, when it is dissolved, pour the must into a demijohn, fit an airlock and ferment out. Rack into a storage jar, add one Campden tablet, seal and store for six months.

Bottle and sweeten to taste with saccharin.

HERBS

The flavouring and sometimes medicinal value of certain herbs has long been known.

A great many books have been published on how to grow and use herbs. Health food shops stock a wide range of herbs for different purposes. One small packet of herbs is usually enough to make one gallon of wine. It must be remembered that herbs contribute only to the bouquet and flavour of a wine, with some trace elements. Everything else has to be added.

Of all herbs, parsley is probably the most popular. It can be used to make a light table wine that accompanies baked fish very well and is also useful for marinading fish. Otherwise, parsley is best used to make a social wine, with a greater quantity of sugar and by fermenting it with a different yeast.

Parsley wines

	Table		*Social*	
Parsley leaves	500g	18 oz	500g	18 oz
Lemons	2		2	
Sultanas	340g	12 oz	500g	18 oz
Sugar	680 g	1½ lb	1 kg	2¼ lb
Water	4 l	7 pt	4 l	7 pt
Yeast	Hock wine		Sauternes wine	
Nutrient				
Campden tablet				

Use young and tender parsley leaves, cut off the stem and use only the leaves. Wash them, cut them up and simmer them together with the thinly pared yellow rind of the lemon (no white pith) for 15 minutes at 80°C (176°F).

When cool, strain out, press dry and discard the pulp; add the washed and chopped sultanas, the expressed and strained juice of the lemon and the activated wine yeast.

Ferment on the pulp for one week, keeping the sultanas well submerged. Strain out the fruit, press it dry, stir in the sugar, pour the must into a demijohn, fit an airlock and ferment out.

Rack into a storage jar, add one Campden tablet and keep for one year before bottling.

Agrimony wine

Agrimony leaves	1 l	1¾ pt
Sultanas	500g	18 oz
Lemons	2	
Sugar	1 kg	2¼ lb
Water	4 l	7 pt
Sauternes wine yeast and nutrient		
Campden tablet		

Use freshly gathered leaves from the plant *Agrimonia eupatorium*, the fragrance of which is not unlike that of the apricot. The leaves are most suitable for making wine in August when the fully grown plants are approaching flowering.

Wash the leaves, shake off the surplus moisture and simmer them for 20 minutes, together with the thinly pared lemon skins. Strain the liquor on to the washed and chopped sultanas and when cool add the expressed and strained lemon juice, nutrient and the activated wine yeast.

Ferment on the pulp for one week, keeping the sultanas pressed down twice each day. Strain out, press dry and discard the sultanas, stir in the sugar, pour the must into a demijohn, fit an airlock and ferment to a finish.

Rack into a storage jar, add one Campden tablet and keep for one year. Sweeten to taste with saccharin if you so wish and serve this wine cool with sweet biscuits.

Angelica wine

There are two versions of this plant; the wild *Angelica sylvestris* and the cultivated *Angelica officinalis*. Gather the flower heads, tender stalks and leaves in April/May. Tisanes and wines made from angelica were reputed to be an aid to digestion, a stimulant to the kidneys, an anti-flatulant and a means of cleansing the blood from impurities.

Angelica	450g	1 lb
Sultanas	500g	18 oz
Lemons	2	
Sugar	1 kg	2¼ lb
Water	4 l	7 pt
Sauternes wine yeast and nutrient		
Campden tablet		

Make in the same way as described for Agrimony

Borage wine

This herb has a salty taste but does not contain sodium. People whose salt intake was restricted used the herb to flavour their food. The herb, *Borago officinalis*, is also reported to be mildly laxative and beneficial to nursing mothers. The blue flowers and tender leaves are used for wine.

Borage flowers and		
leaves	2.8 l	5 pt
Sultanas	500g	18 oz
Lemons	2	
Sugar	1 kg	1¼ lb
Water	4 l	7 pt
Sauternes wine yeast and nutrient		
Campden tablet		

Make in the same way as described for Meadowsweet (p. 83).

Burdock wine

The flowers of this plant were used before hops for flavouring beer. They can also be used for flavouring wine. Burdock flowers combine well with dandelion flowers to make a pleasant summer wine.

Burdock flowers	2 l	3½ pt
Sultanas	500g	18 oz
Lemons	2	
Sugar	1 kg	2¼ lb
Water	4 l	7 pt
Sauternes wine yeast and nutrient		
Campden tablet		

Make in the same way as described for Agrimony (p. 81).

Camomile wine

There are several noxious weeds similar to the camomile herb, *Matricaria camomilla*, so care must be taken in collecting. The camomile flowers have a very pungent but pleasant odour. Use only one cluster containing 15 white flowers. The tisane made from these flowers used to be given to people with some disorder of the kidneys or bladder. It is also said to be an aid to digestion.

Camomile flowers	15	
Lemons	2	
Sultanas	500g	18 oz
Sugar	1 kg	2¼ lb
Water	4 l	7 pt
Sauternes wine yeast and nutrient		
Campden tablet		

Make in the same way as described for Meadowsweet (p. 83).

Lemon balm wine

There are a number of differently scented balms but the most common is lemon (*Melissa officinalis*). When the leaves are rubbed a delicate lemon scent is released. The leaves used to be made into a tisane that had a gentle sedative effect that could dispel a latent headache or symptoms of over-tiredness. Pick the leaves early in the season.

Lemon balm leaves	2.25 l	4 pt
Sultanas	500g	18 oz
Citric acid	10 ml	2 tsp
Sugar	1 kg	2¼ lb
Water	4 l	7 pt
Sauternes wine yeast and nutrient		
Campden tablet		

Make in the same way as described for Agrimony (p. 81), but add the citric acid crystals instead of the lemon juice. Do not use lemons since these make the flavour too pronounced.

Linden wine

An infusion of lime tree flower bracts was once thought to allay digestive and nervous troubles and so induce sleep. They impart a delicate aroma to a wine, the alcohol of which we know to have the same effect as was supposed for the infusion.

Lime flowers and		
bracts	2.8 l	5 pt
Sultanas	500g	18 oz
Citric acid	10 ml	2 tsp
Sugar	1 kg	2¼ lb
Water	4 l	7 pt

Sauternes wine yeast and nutrient
Campden tablet

Remove the stem and any leaves and only use the flowers and bracts.

Make the wine in the same way as described for Agrimony (p. 81) but add the citric acid instead of the lemon juice. Do not use lemons since their flavour would detract from the lime. In recipes where lemons are recommended, the lemon flavour enhances that of the herb.

Lovage aperitif

The whole of this plant (*Ligusticum officinalis*) has culinary uses but only the flowers are used for wine. It makes an interesting aperitif.

Lovage flowers	4 l	7 pt
Sultanas	500g	18 oz
Lemons	2	
Sugar	1 kg	2¼ lb
Water	4 l	7 pt

Sherry wine yeast and nutrient

Pour boiling water over the flowers and rub them against the side of the vessel with the back of a plastic spoon to extract the flavour. Cover and leave to cool.

Strain out, press dry and discard the flowers, and pour the liquor on to the washed and chopped sultanas. Add the thinly pared and chopped rinds of the lemons and the expressed and strained juice. Mix in the activated yeast and nutrient, and ferment in the pulp for 7 days, keeping the floating fruit submerged.

Strain out, press dry and discard the fruit, stir in the sugar and ferment out. Rack into a storage jar but do not top up or add a Campden tablet. Plug the neck of the jar with cotton wool and store for one year.

Meadowsweet table wine

The flowers of this plant (*Spiraea ulmaria*) were once used to make tisanes that were thought to be helpful in relieving kidney troubles and rheumatic pains.

Meadowsweet flowers	4 l	7 pt
Sultanas	500g	18 oz
Lemons	2	
Sugar	1 kg	2¼ lb
Water	4 l	7 pt

Sauternes wine yeast and nutrient
Campden tablet

Pour hot water over the flowers and rub them against the side of the vessel with the back of a plastic spoon to extract the flavour. Cover and leave to cool.

Strain on to the washed and chopped sultanas and the thinly pared and chopped rind of the lemons. Add the expressed and strained lemon juice and the activated yeast and nutrient. Ferment on the pulp for 7 days, keeping the fruit submerged.

Strain out, press dry and discard the pulp, stir in the sugar, pour the must into a demijohn, fit an airlock and ferment out.

Rack into a storage jar, add one Campden tablet and keep for one year.

Mint wine

There are several varieties of this plant (*Mentha*) in addition to the garden variety used for making mint sauce to accompany roast lamb: peppermint, spearmint and apple mint are the best known. Only the tender leaves and tips are used. Discard the stalks.

Mint leaves	1 l	1¾ pt
Sultanas	500g	18 oz
Citric acid	10 ml	2 tsp
Sugar	1 kg	2¼ lb
Water	4 l	7 pt
Sauternes wine yeast and nutrient		
Campden tablet		

Make in the same way as described for Meadowsweet (p. 83), but use citric acid in place of the lemons.

Sage wine

The sage flower from the plant *Salvia officinalis* is sometimes called clary. Traditionally the wine was thought to have aphrodisiacal qualities.

Sage flowers and tips	560 ml	1 pt
Sultanas	500g	18 oz
Lemons	2	
Orange	1	
Sugar	1 kg	2¼ lb
Water	4 l	7 pt
Sauternes wine yeast and nutrient		
Campden tablet		

Collect the florets and tips from the top of the plant, place them in a measuring jug and shake them down but do not press them. Empty them into a bin and add the washed and chopped sultanas, the thinly pared and chopped rind of the lemons and orange (no white pith).

Pour boiling water into the bin, cover and leave to cool. Add the expressed and strained juice of the lemon and orange, then stir in the activated yeast and nutrient.

Ferment on the pulp for five days, keeping the floating solids pressed down twice each day.

Strain out, press dry and discard the pulp, stir in the sugar, pour the must into a demijohn, fit an airlock and ferment to a finish.

Rack into a storage jar, add one Campden tablet, seal and keep for 12 months before bottling.

Sweeten to taste with saccharin as required, and serve this wine cold with a sweet biscuit.

Woodruff wine

A tisane made from this herb (*Galium oderatum*) is reported to promote perspiration and to be helpful to people suffering from a cold in the head. Use only the flowers.

Woodruff flowers	2 l	3½ pt
Sultanas	500g	18 oz
Lemons	2	
Sugar	1 kg	2¼ lb
Water	4 l	7 pt
Sauternes wine yeast and nutrient		
Campden tablet		

Make in the same way as described for Meadowsweet (p. 83).

Yarrow wine

This herb (*Achillea millefolium*) was once used for the treatment of colds and influenza in patients who had a temperature. It is reported to induce perspiration. The flowers have a pleasant smell. Discard the stem.

Yarrow flowers and leaves	4 l	7 pt
Sultanas	500g	18 oz
Lemons	2	
Sugar	1 kg	2¼ lbs
Water	4 l	7 pt
Sauternes wine yeast and nutrient		
Campden tablet		

Make in the same way as described for Meadowsweet (p. 83).

BIRCH SAP

The silver birch (*Betula pendula*) is a graceful tree with a slender trunk covered with a silver white bark, broken with black cracks.

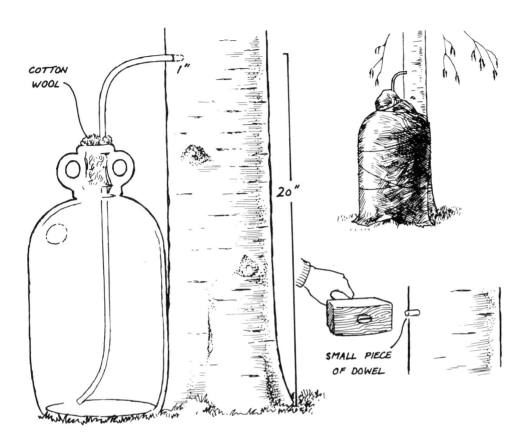

The delicate tracery of the long and pendulant, pencil-thin secondary branches gives the tree a fountain-like appearance. In spring its rising sap can be used as the basis for an interesting wine.

During the first two weeks of March, select a well-grown and mature tree with a trunk some 200 mm (8 in) in diameter. Choose a place on the ground by the bole of the tree where it is suitable to stand a glass demijohn containing one Campden tablet. Drill a small hole through the bark some 25 mm (1 in) deep and 500 mm (20 in) from the ground. Take a plastic tube the same diameter as the hole and push one end into the hole and the other end into the neck of the demijohn. Plug this around with cotton wool, cover the jar with black plastic sheeting and leave it in position, checking from

time to time to see how much sap has entered the jar. After 48 hours or so, some 3.4 litres (approx 6 pints) of sap will have collected and this is enough to take from any one tree. Withdraw the plastic tube from the tree and promptly plug the hole with a piece of dowel rod or good cork, hammered home. That tree should not be sapped again for at least one year.

Birch sap wine

Birch sap	3.4 l	6 pt
Lemons	2	
Oranges	2	
Sugar	1 kg	2¼ lbs
Hock wine yeast and nutrient		
Campden tablet		

Thinly pare the lemons and oranges, place them in a boiling pan, add the birch sap, bring to the boil and simmer for ten minutes

Strain through a sieve into a bin, then discard the peelings.

Stir in the sugar and the strained juices of the oranges and lemons, cover and leave to cool.

Mix in the activated wine yeast, pour the must into a demijohn, fit an airlock and ferment to a finish.

Rack into a storage jar, add one Campden tablet, seal and store for six months.

Serve this wine cool with a sweet biscuit.

NOTE

Sycamore and walnut tree saps may be used in the same way.

10 Avoid these plants

Country people know by tradition those plants that are poisonous or unsafe for eating or making into wine. Town dwellers on a visit to the countryside are less sure of themselves and can easily be taken in by an attractive plant. Others sometimes have an excess of some plant in their garden and are tempted to make wine from it. There is, too, a great urge among amateur winemakers to experiment. Those of us with longer experience, however, urge you to stay with the well-known ingredients and to ignore the doubtful as well as the downright poisonous. An excellent and simple guide is to ask yourself whether you would give the substance to a tiny child to eat. If the answer is 'no', then don't attempt to make wine from it.

The following list is meant as a guide to the more obvious plants to avoid. It is not exhaustive and the fact that the name of a plant is not included does not mean that it is safe. The Ministry of Agriculture and Fisheries has published a more comprehensive guide (*Poisonous Plants in Britain and their effect on animals and man*, HMSO, 1983) and there are a number of semi-scientific books dealing with the causes of the poison and the parts of the plant responsible. The safe rule is '**if in doubt, don't**'.

The word poison is used rather loosely in this context. Ethyl alcohol, the main spirit in wine, mead, beer and cider, is poisonous when consumed in sufficient quantity. A number of other alcohols, even more poisonous, are also present in wines, but in such minute quantities that they do us no harm and even enhance the bouquet and flavour. The use of the word poison, then, doesn't necessarily mean that you would die from drinking wine made from a certain ingredient. But it does mean that you might have a severe headache or stomach upset, or just feel unwell for a short while. Furthermore, it is not just the odd glass of wine that might affect you, but the ingestion of the same wine over a long period during which the poison builds up in your system.

Wine is meant to give us pleasure and to be enjoyed. Experiment if you wish with blending safe and well-known ingredients in unusual combinations, but **do avoid the following, and any other plant about which you are not certain**.

A
Acacia, aconite, alder, anemone, aquilegia, azalea.
B
Baneberry, bay tree leaves, beech nuts, belladonna, berberis, bindweed, bitter almond, black nightshade, bluebell, box tree leaves, broom, bryony, buckthorn, buddleia, buttercup.
C
Campion, celandine, charlock, chrysanthemum, cineraria, clematis, clover, columbine, cotoneaster, cow-bane, crocus, crowfoot, cuckoo-pint, cyclamen.
D
Daffodil, dahlia, deadly nightshade, delphinium, dwarf elder.

Avoid these plants

F
Figwort, fool's parsley, foxglove, fungi of all kinds.
G
Geranium, gladiolus, goosefoot, green potatoes.
H
All members of the hellebore family, hemlock, henbane, holly, honeysuckle (both flowers and berries), horse chestnut flowers and conkers, hydrangea, hyacinth.
I
Iris, ivy.
J
Jasmine, jonquil.
L
Laburnum, laurel, lilac, lilies of the valley, lilies of all kinds, lobelia, lucerne, lupins.
M
Marsh marigolds, meadow rue, mezereon, mistletoe, monkshood.

N
Narcissus.
O
Orchids.
P
Peony, pheasant's eye, poppy, privet.
R
Ragwort, rhododendron, rhubarb leaves.
S
Snowdrop, spearwort, spindleberries, spurge, sweet pea.
T
Thorn apple, tobacco plant, tomato stems and leaves, traveller's joy, tulip.
W
Wood anemone, woody nightshade.
Y
Yew.

II Liqueurs

Liqueurs and ratafias were much more widely made in the home during the seventeenth and eighteenth centuries than they are today. In those days, spirits of all kinds were very cheap and many homes had their own alembic for making them, but it is illegal to make spirits at home today. There is good evidence, however, to indicate that the making of liqueurs at home is on the increase by simple and not too expensive methods.

INSTANT LIQUEURS

For those who want to make a liqueur in a quick and easy way, the T. Noirot concentrated liqueur essences are available from France and can be bought from most Home Brew shops. The 20 ml phial of essence is sufficient to flavour one litre of liqueur. Experience shows that they are mostly best used in conjunction with vodka rather than any other spirit. The apricot, peach and morello cherry brandies, however, may be used with the French 'Eau de vie pour les fruits'. Although this has a brandy taste, it is colourless and free from the caramel flavouring so often used to colour ordinary brandy. Vodka is otherwise preferred because it is colourless and tasteless and doesn't vary the flavour of the essence.

Although commercial liqueurs are sometimes very strong, many of them are much less so, and one litre of vodka is often enough to make 3 or 4 bottles of the less strong styles. In addition to the spirit you will need some bland, sweet and strong white wine, assorted bottles of essence of your choice, some quick-dissolving sugar and some glycerine. For those who can obtain some from their chemist, a few drops of capsicum tincture are beneficial. This ingredient is not packed for sale, but if you explain to a pharmacist that you want only about 20 mls for adding to home-made liqueurs, the chances are that he/she will let you have this much from their bulk stock.

The only equipment required is a jug, spoon and bottle. The quantity of sugar needed depends on the sweetness of the wine used. It is likely to vary from 170g (6 oz) to 250g (9 oz). The quantity of vodka to use varies with the strength of the liqueur being made and the strength of the wine available. Somewhere between 250 and 340 ml (9 fl oz to 12 fl oz) of vodka is usually enough.

Place 170g (6 oz) sugar in the jug, pour on 250 ml (9 fl oz) of the vodka. Add about three-quarters of the essence and stir in about half a pint of wine. Stir gently until all the sugar is dissolved. Now taste the liqueur. It is possible that more sugar, or essence, or vodka or wine will be required and this can now be added to suit your taste. It is so much easier to add a little more of an ingredient than it is to reduce an excess.

When you feel that you have the balance about right, stir in one dessertspoonful of glycerine and ten single drops of capsicum tincture. Taste the liqueur again and, if needs be, add a further teaspoonful or so of glycerine and one or two more drops of tincture. The glycerine adds a rich smoothness to the liqueur and the capsicum tincture imparts a warm glow that gives the impression of a greater spirit content. As soon as you have adjusted the liqueur to suit your taste it is ready for serving. It improves a little if it is bottled and kept for about one week to homogenise.

FRUIT LIQUEURS

The best-known liqueur from the country-side is sloe gin, but other fruits can also be used to make very enjoyable liqueurs that can be used not only for drinking after dinner but also for flavouring ice creams, sweet pancakes, trifles and other desserts. Little equipment is needed beyond a large kilner-type jar and some fancy bottles. The spirits are undoubtedly expensive but can some-times be obtained a little more cheaply in duty free shops or on special offers from wine and spirit stores. The only other ingredients you will need are the sugar for sweetening and the fruits you gather. These should be the very best obtainable, fully ripe, large, juicy and unblemished.

Sloe gin

Selected black-ripe sloes	340g	12 oz
Granulated white sugar	250g	9 oz
Gin	625 ml	22 fl oz

Remove the stalks, wash the sloes, prick them all over with a pastry fork or bodkin, and place them in a jar with the sugar sprinkled over them in layers. Pour on the gin, seal the jar and place it in an available position. Shake the jar every day or so for three months, until all the sugar is dissolved and the colour and flavour have been leached out of the sloes.

Open the jar, pour the liqueur through a nylon sieve into a funnel fitted to a standard size, screw-stoppered spirit bottle. Press the sloes to squeeze out the remaining liqueur, discard them and seal the bottle. Label the bottle 'Sloe Gin', add the date and store for nine months.

NOTE

Selected damsons may be used instead of sloes. Cut them in half and remove the stones. Make the liqueur in the same way, but drain the damsons dry and do not press them. Serve them on a pastry flan with cream as an outstanding dessert.

Blackcurrant rum

Selected black-ripe blackcurrants	250g	9 oz
Granulated white sugar	340g	12 oz
White rum	560 ml	1 pt

Stalk and wash the blackcurrants, crush them and place them in a large bowl or jug. Sprinkle on and mix in the sugar, and then the rum.

Stir gently until the sugar is completely dissolved, then cover and leave for 24 hours.

Strain out the fruit, gently press it, pour the liqueur into a standard size, screw-stoppered spirit bottle, label it and leave it for six months to mature.

Do not use brown rum because it contains caramel that distorts the flavour of the currants.

Mix the blackcurrants into ice cream, fruit salad or a trifle.

Apricot brandy

Selected ripe apricots	10	
White sugar	200g	7 oz
Eau de vie pour les fruits	625 ml	22 fl oz

Stalk and wash the apricots, remove the stones and cut the fruit into thin slices. Place these in a jar with the sugar in layers, then pour on the eau de vie. This is a colourless brandy widely available in France for this purpose. Seal the jar and leave it in an available position so that it can be shaken every day or so for three months.

Strain the liqueur into a standard size, screw-stoppered spirit bottle, draining the apricot slices dry but not pressing them. Seal the bottle, label and store it for six months. Serve the apricot slices with cream, or mix them into a fruit salad or trifle.

NOTE
Peaches may be used instead of apricots, but peel them first.

Blackberry beauty

Selected large		
black-ripe berries	340g	12 oz
Granulated white sugar	250g	9 oz
Eau de vie pour les		
fruits *or* Vodka	625 ml	22 fl oz

Stalk and wash the blackberries, cut them in half (longways) with a very sharp knife or razor blade, place them in a jar and sprinkle them with sugar in layers. Pour on the eau de vie pour les fruits or the vodka, seal the jar and leave it in a position where it can be gently shaken every day or so for two months.

Open the jar, pour the blackberries into a large nylon sieve and drain the liqueur through a funnel into a standard size, screw-stoppered spirit bottle. Label and store for nine months. Serve the blackberries with cream, or whisk them into a fool.

NOTE
Loganberries, mulberries, raspberries and strawberries may be used instead of black-berries. If the liqueur is not sweet enough for your palate, stir in some more sugar at the bottling stage.

Summer fruits liqueur

An interesting liqueur can be made in a similar way to the summer fruit wine. Use any, or all, of the summer fruits, especially strawberries, raspberries and dessert gooseberries, sweet cherries, ripe peaches, ripe Victoria plums and even a ripe pear or two.

Use a large glazed earthenware, ceramic or china vessel with a capacity of 2.5 to 3 litres (4½ to 5¼ pints). Use about 340g (12 oz) of each fruit as it comes into season. Remove stalks, wash the fruit and drain it as dry as you can in a colander. Remove any stones or cut larger fruits into smaller pieces as necessary. Lay the fruit in a flat bowl or square-shaped plastic box, and cover it with sugar using half as much sugar as you have fruit, i.e. 170g (6 oz), cover the fruit and leave overnight, then empty it into the large container and cover it with a dark rum.

After adding more fruit and sugar, add more rum and if the fruit rises then keep it submerged with a china saucer or plate and make sure that there is always about 6 mm (¼ in) of rum above the fruit.

Use rum that is from 95–103° proof spirit, 56% alcohol, and when the jar is full leave it for at least three months. Keep the pot covered at all times with Clingfilm, or the like, to keep out flies and insects.

Strain off the liqueur as required and serve the fruit with ice cream or in fruit salad.

12 Mead, melomels and metheglyns

There is evidence that honey, probably from colonies of wild bees, was known to mankind some 10,000 years before Christ. It seems most likely, also, that a weak natural mead was known and perhaps even made. Some honey diluted with water and left in an open vessel would soon begin to ferment and taste quite different from water or diluted honey. Wine from grape juice came some 2,000 years later and ale somewhat later still.

We do not know when mead or ale was first drunk in Britain but both were well developed before the Romans came in 54 B.C. The Celts were fond of mead and often added herbs to the fermenting brew, as well as crushed apples!

The Saxons, who came to Britain after the Romans had left, brought with them im-

proved methods of beekeeping; mead was a very popular drink for them. The spread of Christianity and the growth of monasteries and convents increased the need for keeping bees, since the wax was used for making candles and polishing furniture. The honey was used for sweetening fruit and cakes as well as for making into mead.

For many centuries mead was the wine of poor people. It was drunk on special occasions, in particular at wedding festivities. Indeed, it is thought that our word 'honeymoon' derived from the drinking of mead for 28 days after a wedding. It continued to be very popular through the days of 'Merry England', right up to the end of the eighteenth century. Every landowner brewed both mead and ale for his family and estate workers. Many books appeared between 1700 and 1800 giving recipes for making mead with different flavours. The different honeys were discussed and also different methods of making mead. But people were already moving from the country to towns, new beverages were becoming fashionable and the making of mead began to wane. It never died out completely because bees are such fascinatingly interesting insects. There will always be beekeepers.

Interest in making mead was re-awakened with the home winemaking movement which began in 1945. Science has now taught us what honey contains and how we can adjust the must with acid, nitrogen, phosphate and tannin to make better meads than in the past.

An average honey contains about 77% sugar and 17½% water. The remaining 5½% consists of salts of iron, phosphorus, lime, sodium, potassium, sulphate and manganese, with traces of citric, formic, malic, succinic and amino acids, together with dextrin, pollen, oils, gums, waxes, fats, yeast enzymes, vitamins, albumen, protein and ash.

The flavour of honey depends on the source from which the bees obtain the nectar. English honey is said to be the best in the world, perhaps because it so often contains a mixture of nectars. Foreign honey is sometimes obtained exclusively from a single source. Of these, one of the most interesting for mead is orange-blossom honey. This makes a splendid dry table mead with a fragrant scent of oranges. Another is clover honey, which makes a distinguished dessert mead. A third is acacia honey.

Adding other ingredients to a honey solution to vary the flavour of the mead is a very old custom. The most popular variations are as follows.

Cyser A mixture of honey and apple juice, thought to be very beneficial in promoting good health.

Pyment A mixture of honey and grape juice. The honey was originally added to poor-quality grapes, low in sugar. The grapes added essential acid to the honey and made a harmonious blend.

Melomel A mixture of honey with any fruit or flower. The meadmaker would add whatever was available. Blackcurrant melomel is very nutritious but any sharp-tasting fruit will do. Elderflower and rose petals are the most popular of the flower melomels. At one time violets were widely used.

Metheglin A mixture of honey flavoured with herbs or spices. This beverage was thought to be particularly advantageous to sick people who benefited both from the therapeutic qualities of the herbs and the nutrition of the honey. Both herbs and spices taste very bitter in a dry mead and in my opinion metheglin should always be finished sweet.

Hypocras A mixture of honey, herbs and grape juice. It is said that this beverage got its name from Hypocrates, the Father of Medicine, who used to strain out the medicinal herbs through the sleeve of his gown. Obviously, a beneficial mead but another that needs to be served sweet.

Indeed, most meads need to be finished at least slightly sweet. When all the sugar in honey is fermented out the flavour changes significantly. The one exception known to me is orange-blossom honey, although even this tastes slightly better with a final specific gravity of 1.000, rather than 0.992.

Mead can be made dry enough to be suitable for drinking at table with roast poultry or ham, or sweet enough to accompany puddings. It can also be sparkled in the same way as a wine. But mead really tastes best when served cold and slightly sweet on its own. Then you can smell the fragrance of the nectar and enjoy the flavour of the honey.

Metheglins taste superb when mulled and sweetened with more honey.

When diluting the honey it is necessary to use warm water. Some meadmakers advocate the boiling of the solution and the skimming off of any scum that may arise.

This is less necessary than it used to be and even for a locally produced honey a gentle simmer for five minutes is usually quite enough. Should any scum appear, remove and discard it. Cool the must to between 15° and 20°C (59° to 68°F). Because of the absence of acid, 4 or 5 level teaspoonfuls of citric and tartaric or malic acid should be added – or better still a mixture of all three. Nutrient salts are also essential for a good fermentation since honey lacks nitrogen and phosphate.

Any wine yeast will ferment a honey solution. The best results, however, have been obtained using a German wine yeast or a Sauternes wine yeast. Fermentation should be started at a temperature around 24°C (75°F) and as soon as it is flourishing, the jar should be moved to a cooler temperature, around 18°C (65°F). Fermentation will continue for up to six weeks, although it is usually over in three or four. Sometimes it continues very slowly for up to six months. Sufficient acid, nutrient and an even temperature are essential for a good fermentation.

Sometimes mead is ready to drink almost as soon as it is racked and bright. On other occasions it can take two or three years to mature. It needs to be served cool to the taste, but not cold, as this reduces the flavour. In the sixteenth and seventeenth centuries mead used to be served from a mazer. This is a large wooden bowl, sometimes carved from a piece of bird's-eye maple and embellished with filigree silver work. Such a mazer might have three handles and be passed from one person to another to drink. A simple mazer might only have the owner's name engraved on it, a custom followed in some monasteries.

Dry table mead

Cream set honey	1.25 kg	2¾ lb
Citric acid	20 ml	4 tsp
Grape tannin	3 ml	½ tsp
Nutrient salts	5 ml	1 tsp
Water	3.7 l	6½ pt
Hock wine yeast		
Campden tablet		

Dissolve the honey, acid and tannin in hot water (80°C, 176°F), cover and leave to cool. Mix in the nutrient salts and an activated yeast. Pour the must into a sterilised glass demijohn, fit an airlock and ferment out.

Rack the mead into a sterilised storage jar, top up with cold boiled water, add one Campden tablet, seal, label and store until bright. Rack again and mature for at least one year.

Sweet table mead

Brown loose honey	1.5 kg	3½ lb
Citric acid	20 ml	4 tsp
Grape tannin	5 ml	1 tsp
Nutrient salts	5 ml	1 tsp
Water	3.7 l	6½ pt
Sauternes wine yeast		
Potassium sorbate	1g	¼ tsp
Campden tablet		

METHOD A

Make the mead as described for dry table mead, but after ten days has elapsed from the start of fermentation, check the specific gravity every three days. When the reading reaches 1.020, stir in one gram of potassium sorbate and one crushed Campden tablet. Move the jar to a cold place or leave it in the refrigerator overnight. Next day filter the mead (to remove all the yeast) into a freshly sterilised jar and, if necessary, top up with cold boiled water. Seal the jar, label and store for one year.

METHOD B

Using only 1.25 kg (2¾ lb) of brown loose honey make a dry mead as already described. When you wish to drink your mead, empty one bottle of it into a carafe or decanter and sweeten it with 56g (2 oz) of brown loose honey. Stir gently to ensure a thorough mix of mead and honey, then serve it in tulip-shaped glasses.

This method prevents all possible risk of refermentation and avoids having to filter the fermenting mead and adding potassium sorbate.

NOTE
Both the dry and the sweet mead will contain about 12% alcohol.

Dessert mead

Brown loose honey	2 kg	4½ lb
Citric acid	25 ml	5 tsp
Grape tannin	5 ml	1 tsp
Water	3.4 l	6 pt
Nutrient	5 ml	1 tsp
Tokay wine yeast		

Dissolve 1.35 kg (3 lb) of the honey, together with the acid and tannin in hot water (80°C, 176°F), cover and leave to cool. Stir in the activated yeast and the nutrient, pour the must into a demijohn and fit an airlock. Leave to ferment in a temperature of 24°C (75°F).

After ten days, remove some must from the jar, stir in one-third of the remaining honey, making sure that it is well dissolved before returning the must to the jar.

Repeat this after a further five days with half the remaining honey, and again with the final portion of honey after a further five days.

When fermentation is finished and the mead begins to clear, rack into a sterilised jar, top up with cold boiled water, seal and store until the mead is bright.

Rack again and store for two years or longer. This mead is very strong and should be sweetened if necessary with more honey.

Cyser

Cream set honey	1 kg	2¼ lb
Apple juice	1 l	1¾ pt
Citric acid	15 ml	3 tsp
Grape tannin	3 ml	½ tsp
Nutrient salts	5 ml	1 tsp
Water	2.7 l	4¾ pt
Champagne wine yeast		
Campden tablet		

Make as for a dry mead (p. 94), adding the apple juice with the yeast.

A sweet cyser can be made as described for a sweet mead, with the addition of apple juice.

Alternatively, honey may be added to the recipe for apple wine (p. 38). Add 450g (1 lb) cream set honey instead of 340g (12 oz) white sugar.

Pyment

Cream set honey	1.25 kg	2¾ lb
Citric acid	15 ml	3 tsp
Grape tannin	3 ml	½ tsp
Nutrient salts	5 ml	1 tsp
White grape juice	600 ml	21 fl oz
Water	2.1 l	3¾ pt
Hock wine yeast		
Campden tablet		

Make as for a dry mead, adding the bottle of grape juice with the yeast.

A sweet pyment can be made as described for a sweet mead. Alternatively, honey may be added to a grape must instead of sugar. Use 450g (1 lb) cream set honey in place of 340g (¾ lb) sugar.

Red grape juice may be used to make a rosé pyment.

Melomel

Brown loose honey	1.35 kg	3 lb
Blackcurrants	250g	9 oz
Water	3.7 l	6½ pt
Citric acid	10 ml	2 tsp
Grape tannin	5 ml	1 tsp
Nutrient salts	5 ml	1 tsp
Maury yeast		
Campden tablet		

Dissolve the honey, acid and tannin in hot water (80°C, 176°F) and when cool add the washed, stalked and crushed blackcurrants, together with the nutrient salts and activated yeast. Cover the vessel and ferment on the pulp for three days, keeping the blackcurrants submerged or pressed down twice daily.

Strain out, press dry and discard the blackcurrant skins, pour the must into a sterilised demijohn, fit an airlock and ferment out.

Rack into a storage jar, top up, add one Campden tablet, seal, label and store until the melomel is bright, then rack again and keep for one year. Sweeten with honey just before serving.

Other fruits suitable for making into melomels in the same way are:

Bilberry	220g	8 oz
Blackberry	450g	1 lb
Damsons	450g	1 lb
Gooseberry	450g	1 lb
Loganberry	220g	8 oz
Mulberry	220g	8 oz
Raspberry	220g	8 oz
Redcurrants	220g	8 oz
Rhubarb	450g	1 lb
Orange juice	1 l	1¾ pt
(make as for cyser)		
Pineapple juice	1 l	1¾ pt
(make as for cyser)		

Alternatively, 450g (1 lb) brown loose honey may be added to any wine recipe in place of 340g (¾ lb) sugar.

Herb metheglin

Brown loose honey	1.8 kg	4 lb
Citric acid	20 ml	4 tsp
Water	3.4 l	6 pt
Nutrient	5 ml	1 tsp
Bouquet garni of herbs	56g	2 oz
such as rosemary, thyme,		
bay leaves and marjoram		
Sauternes wine yeast		

Dissolve the honey and acid in hot water (80°C, 176°F), cover and leave to cool. Mix in the nutrient and an activated yeast, then pour the must into a demijohn. Fit an airlock and leave in a warm place, 24°C (75°F), until fermentation is vigorous, then move to a cooler place, 18°C (65°F). Place the herbs in a large-mesh nylon bag and suspend this in the must for three days. The herbs should be loose and free in the nylon, not tightly packed, otherwise it will be difficult to diffuse the flavours. Suspend them on a cotton passed through the airlock in such a way that they are in the centre of the jar. After their removal, continue fermentation until it stops.

Rack the clearing mead from its sediment, top up with cold boiled water, seal, label and store until the metheglin is bright, then rack again and mature for two years.

Spice metheglin

Instead of herbs, a sachet of spices may be used. The following are recommended but may be varied to suit your taste:

1 large piece of dried root ginger	crushed
12 whole cloves	crushed
1 stick cinnamon	crushed
1 lemon, thinly pared rind only	chopped

Make the metheglin in the same way as just described, suspending the nylon or muslin bag of spices in the same manner and for the same length of time.

Hypocras

Brown loose honey	1.5 kg	3½ lb
Grape juice (red or white)	600 ml	21 fl oz
Water	2 l	3½ pt
Citric acid	15 ml	3 tsp
Nutrient	5 ml	1 tsp
Bouquet garni of herbs or spices (see metheglin 1 and 2)		
Sauternes wine yeast		
Campden tablet		

Start off the hypocras in the same way as for a pyment (p. 95). When the fermentation is going well, suspend the herbs or spices in it in the same manner as for a metheglin (see above). When fermentation finishes, rack the hypocras from the sediment, add one Campden tablet, top up, seal and store until it is bright. Rack again. Keep for two years, then sweeten with honey, if necessary, just before serving.

Sparkling mead

Cream set honey	1 kg	2¼ lb
Citric acid	15 ml	3 tsp
Grape tannin	3 ml	½ tsp
Nutrient salts	5 ml	1 tsp
Water	3.7 l	6½ pt
Champagne wine yeast		
Campden tablet		
Cream set honey	85g	3 oz
Champagne wine yeast		

Make the mead in the same way as described for a dry table mead (p. 94). After it has matured for six months or more, mix in the additional 3 oz honey and the second champagne yeast. Fit an airlock and move the jar to a warm place, 30°C (86°F), for a few hours until fermentation starts.

Siphon the fermenting mead into six champagne bottles, leaving a gap of 5 cm (2 in) from the top of the mead to the mouth of the bottle. Fit softened hollow-domed plastic stoppers and wire cages.

Lay the bottles on their sides and leave them in a warm place for one week. Transfer them to a cool store for one year, keeping the bottles still on their sides.

Before serving, disgorge the sediment as described for wine (p. 34). Don't forget the saccharin.

VINEGAR

It is very easy to make vinegar from beer, cider, mead and wine. For beer and cider simply half fill a gallon jar, add one pint of vinegar, plug the neck of the jar with cotton wool and leave it in a warm place for three months. Mead and wine should be diluted – two pints of mead or wine with two pints of cold water. Add one pint of vinegar and continue as described for beer and cider.

After three months, carefully siphon the new vinegar into screw stoppered bottles, then stand them on a cloth in the bottom of a fish kettle or preserving pan. Fill the pan with water to the level of the vinegar in the bottles and bring the water to the boil. Simmer for 20 minutes, then screw on the caps and remove the bottles from the water. When cool, tighten the caps, label and use as required.

The important principles are:

1 Do not use a base stronger than 6% alcohol.

2 Leave plenty of air space in the jar and plug lightly with cotton wool.

3 Sterilise the new vinegar before use.

13 Cider

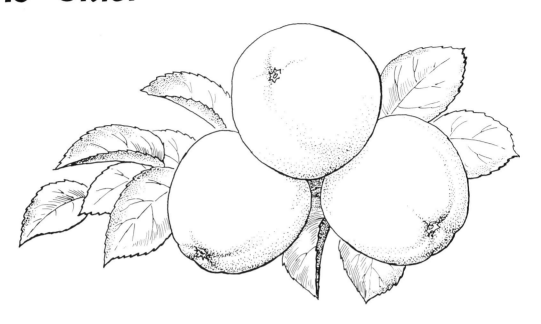

The story that everything that exists evolved from atoms of carbon, hydrogen and oxygen stretches the imagination to unmentionable lengths when it comes to beverages as natural and as splendid as wine and cider and mead. I can accept that apple trees as we know them were developed over the centuries from trees that grew in a wild, unkempt and uncared for state. I find it hard to believe that some Omnipotent Creator did not have a hand in making the first apple tree or the first vine. If so, then we should express gratitude to the Deity for providing us with so many good fruits from which we can make beverages that not only give us enjoyment but are also beneficial to our health.

Knowledge of cider goes back at least to Biblical days, for our modern word cider was evolved from the ancient Hebrew word *shekar*. The Romans used the word *sicera* and the French turned that into *sidre*. The old English word was *sicer* and meant any intoxicating liquor. Indeed, there has been for generations a belief that old English vineyards were not in fact vineyards but cider orchards.

Be that as it may, cider apples are quite different from eating or cooking apples. They are sour, bitter and rough to the tongue. It seems almost certain that the knowledge of how to press the juice from grapes was used in the crushing and pressing of apples. If you have an abundance of small apples (as they then were) and no grapes, an imaginative person with knowledge of the making of wine would certainly try to make some apple 'wine'.

Experience soon showed the kinds of apples that produced the best drink, and blending of the different varieties improved the quality still further.

Cider apples grew abundantly in south-east England and in the West Country from Devonshire to Herefordshire. In 1676, we learn from John Worlidge, the cider made in Herefordshire was taken to London and valued above the wine from France. He was an expert cidermaker and designed a mill for crushing and pressing the apples that has hardly changed.

There are three important factors in cider-making. First, get your apple blend well balanced. You need 4 parts sweet apples to 2 parts sharp and 1 part bitter. You also need some well-flavoured fruit, for the cider will otherwise lack flavour.

Second, wash the ripe and mellow fruit free from stones, grass, leaves, twigs and weed. Pick out any damaged or diseased fruit and discard it. Use only sound ripe fruit if you want to make good cider, otherwise your effort is wasted.

Third, protect the crushed fruit and press-ed juice from the air with sulphur dioxide. Apples are prone to turn brown as soon as they are cut or crushed and this can produce a taint in the finished cider. Similarly with the juice: if it is not protected it will oxidise and taint the cider.

Commercial cidermakers use a mixture of different apples that can be allocated into four groups: sweet, bitter-sweet, bitter-sharp, sharp. When possible they use 3 measures of sweet and bitter-sweet apples to 1 measure of bitter-sharp and sharp. They use varieties by such names as Chisel-Jersey, Coates-Jersey, Dabinette, Michelin, Stem-bridge-Jersey and Yarlington Mill.

These are rarely available to the home cidermaker, who must use more or less of whatever is available. The basic need is for sweet eating apples to produce the sugar for conversion into alcohol, but this would taste medicinal if no sour cooking apples were included, for acid is the cornerstone of bouquet and flavour. Some bitter crab apples and green pears are needed, too, for tannin that produces character to the cider. It is clearly a waste of time trying to make cider from a single variety of apple. If you have only the fruit of one tree available to you, try to swap some with a neighbour. The more varieties that you can muster in the different groups the better will be the cider, but at least get the group proportions right.

As an aid to cidermakers, several manufac-turers now produce cans containing 1 kg of concentrated cider apple juice from France. The flavour is somewhat mild but it makes an excellent additive to a home-made cider. Commercially, the best ciders are usually a blend of several different ciders, just as many of the best wines are a blend of other wines or the same wine from other years. It is rarely possible for home cidermakers to blend their ciders, but the addition of some cider con-centrate goes some way to meet this need. A few cartons of pure apple juice from the supermarket could also be added to increase the complexity.

If you are travelling in Devon, Somerset, Gloucestershire, Worcestershire or Here-fordshire in the early autumn, it is worth trying to get a bag of mixed cider apples. Most of us need something like 9 kg (20 lb) of apples to make a gallon of cider. Regard that quantity as the minimum and stretch it with cooking and eating apples, some crab apples or hard green pears, a can of concentrated cider juice and a few cartons of apple juice. It should not be too difficult to build up enough ingredients to make a five-gallon batch. It is important when making cider to understand the principles, and to formulate your own recipe from the ingredients available to you. Unlike beer, mead and wine, the ingredients of a cider recipe are rarely available to more than a few other people. Even so, here are some suggestions for five-gallon batches.

Cider

1 Sweet and bitter-sweet
cider apples   30 kg   68 lb
Bitter-sharp and sharp
cider apples   10 kg   22 lb

2 Mixed cider apples   18 kg   40 lb
Mixed eating apples   13.5 kg   30 lb
Mixed cooking apples   6.75 kg   15 lb
Crab apples   2.27 kg   5 lb

3 Mixed eating apples   20 kg   45 lb
Mixed cooking apples   9 kg   20 lb
Crab apples   4 kg   9 lb
Concentrated cider
juice   1 kg   2¼ lb
Water (approx.)   4.5 l   1 gal

4 Mixed eating apples   13.5 kg   30 lb
Mixed cooking apples   9 kg   20 lb
Crab apples   4 kg   9 lb
Concentrated cider
juice   1 kg   2¼ lb
Cartons of pure apple
juice   4 l   7 pt
Water (approx.)   4.5 l   1 gal

Having washed and mellowed the fruit, crush it as best you can. There are a number of different ways and you must choose that most convenient to you.

1 Use a proper apple crusher such as can be bought from specialised suppliers of larger equipment for home winemakers and small commercial concerns.

2 Use a stainless steel blade attached to a shaft that fits into an electric drill. Pass the shaft through the lid of a polythene bin, place the apples in the bin, attach the lid, switch on and move the blade up and down in the bin until the contents are adequately crushed. It helps if you quarter the apples first and drop them into a sulphite solution before crushing.

3 Use a block of hardwood attached to a broom handle and stomp this down on to the apples time and time again until the apples are crushed. It helps if you crush only a fairly thin layer of apples at a time.

4 Place some apples in a polythene bag and hit them with a mallet or rolling pin. This method is a bit slow, since only a dozen or so apples can be crushed at a time.

5 Cut the apples into quarters or eighths, drop them into a sulphite solution as you do so, drain them, pack them into polythene bags and freeze them. After a few days remove them from the freezer, thaw them and they will crush more easily.

6 Coarsely grate or mince the apples – a slow business likely to cause browning and spoilage.

7 Liquidise them. Even slower for such a large quantity.

The apples need to be finely crushed, otherwise the juice cannot be expressed. As soon as possible mix in sodium or potassium metabisulphite to the crushed fruit. One crushed Campden tablet per 4 kg (9 lb) fruit is adequate. Also add one 5 ml spoonful of a pectic enzyme per 4 kg (9 lb). Keep the bin full and well covered to exclude air. Even so press out the juice as quickly as you can.

A strong press is essential – the larger the better. Pack the fruit into a sterilised hessian or coarse linen bag and place this in the press. Apply pressure evenly at first until all the slack has been taken up, then pause until the flow becomes a trickle, then apply more pressure. When there seems to be no more juice in the apples, open the press and either turn the bag upside down or mix up the apples. Apply pressure again and plenty of juice will flow. Repeat this process, turning the bag on its sides or churning up the apples until a firm 'cake' has been formed that can be handled without breaking.

Commercial cidermakers pre-fill their containers with carbon dioxide or nitrogen. This excludes the air so that the cider juice is protected from oxidation. If you have an empty plastic beer keg fitted with a CO_2 injector, you could at least part fill a keg with two or three squirts of gas which, being heavier than air, would sink to the bottom of the keg. Then remove the cap so that the air can escape and start filling the keg with juice straight from the press. It helps if this is funnelled into a plastic tube, the end of which just touches the bottom of the keg and so is beneath the CO_2.

When all the juice has been expressed and the keg is full, replace the cap and leave for 24 hours while the pectic enzyme degrades the pectin and the sulphur dioxide diminishes.

Commercial cidermakers use a yeast called *Saccharomyces elipsoideus uvarum* but this is not likely to be available and a champagne wine yeast makes an excellent alternative. Activate it in tepid water before use. Before mixing it into the juice, however, check the specific gravity for this can vary with the season as well as with the fruit varieties. A minimum reading of 1.046 is required. If this is not achieved naturally, then sufficient sugar should be added to raise the gravity to an appropriate level. Do not add too much, however, otherwise the cider will become too strong; 1.054 is an upper limit for a dry cider. If a sweet cider is desired, it is better to make a dry cider and then sweeten it just before serving.

The fermentation of cider is similar to that of white wine. Use an airlock and as soon as the fermentation is under way move the vessel to a slightly cooler place, say 16°C (61°F) or cooler still as long as you can maintain activity. A slow fermentation in a cool atmosphere improves the flavour of the cider.

When fermentation is finished, rack the cider from its lees as you would a wine, add one crushed Campden tablet per gallon to inhibit oxidation and prevent infection, then mature it in bulk for three or four months before bottling. Screw-stoppered bottles are normally used and if the cider is too dry for your taste, add one crushed saccharin tablet to each bottle. Store the cider in a cool place and serve it cool. It is ready for drinking in about six months and does not normally keep beyond the year.

Cider is an excellent thirst-quenching drink with all the traditional nourishment of the apple. It has alcohol, mineral salts, vitamins and acids – especially malic acid, long thought to be good for cleansing the kidneys. It makes a splendid companion for ham sandwiches, for baked or boiled ham, indeed pork in any form. It is also used in cooking pork.

Cider may be sparkled in the same way as wine, or made into vinegar. It is becoming increasingly popular with young people, but it should always be remembered that it is half as strong again as beer!

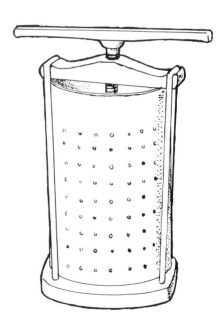

14 Home-brewed beers of every style

INTRODUCTION

No one knows just how brewing began, but we do know from archaeological sources that brewing beer from barley was already widely practised some 5,000 years before the birth of Christ, both in Egypt and Chaldea. It was seen as some sort of luxury, for an Egyptian papyrus contains details of a barley-wine tax collected in the city of Memphis on the Nile as early as 3,400 BC. A recipe for brewing barley-wine (it was not yet called beer) was found inscribed on a Babylonian cuneiform library brick dated 2,800 BC, and the first mention of a public beer-house is on a Babylonian clay tablet dated 2,225 BC.

The knowlege of brewing spread throughout the Middle East via the Egyptians through the Greeks (who called this brew *zythos*) to the Romans (who called their brew *cerevisa*). But by the time the Romans arrived in Britain, the Celts were already making the same brew which they called *courmi*. The beer was usually drunk without additional flavouring, but in England burdock, yarrow, nettle or spruce might be added. Hops were disliked quite strongly by Britons.

The *Book of the Ancient Laws of Ireland*, dated 438 AD, details precise regulations controlling the growing and malting of barley and the brewing of beer, called 'coirm', from it. Ale, for soon it was so called, from

the Anglo-Saxon 'aelu', benefited from the orderly life of the monasteries. The monks improved the quality of the malt and the method of brewing. As a result the beer became a little stronger, better flavoured and less frequently sour. Drunkenness became widespread. Decrees were issued time and again by different abbots, as well as by Theodore the seventh Archbishop of Canterbury, stating the penalties that a monk would suffer were he to be found drunk. Kings acted regarding the general populace, notably King Ine (693 AD). Later King Edgar (959–75 AD) decreed the closure of many ale-houses, allowing only one for each village.

By now, the brewing of ale had become the prerogative of women who both baked and brewed, using the same balm (yeast) for each.

The word ale continued to be used for another 500 years to describe the beverage made from fermenting a solution prepared from malted barley, although frequently other cereals, especially wheat, were used as well as, or instead of, barley. It was only when the brew was flavoured with hops that it was called beer.

Brewing continued to be the work of every housewife but some women, perhaps those widows who needed to earn money to maintain their family, brewed more than they needed and sold their surplus. Some, no doubt, became the owners of ale-houses and earned the name ale-wife. Ale was a very important commodity and on special occasions the sale of ale would be reserved exclusively in aid of some local need, perhaps the repair of a church (church-ale) or of a bridge (bridge-ale).

Henry II levied the first tax in England on ale in 1188 and Henry III regularised the prices paid for given quantities. In an ale-house a person would buy, say, half a gallon (or more) of an ale and then pour it as required into his own stoup or mug, or into those of his friends!

That ale-wives still controlled the business is clear from the record dated 1327 of a survey of the 252 tradespeople who paid taxes in the little town of Faversham in Kent. Of the 84 brewers, all were women! But the next 200 years saw slow changes. Hops were introduced not only to flavour the beer but also to help preserve it. In 1524, Flemish immigrants settled in Kent, planted their hops and began an industry that still flourishes there today. Men were now taking over the brewing, building brew-houses and brewing larger quantities. By 1591, 26,400 barrels of beer were despatched from the London docks, mostly to the Baltic States. In the following century the tax on beer was so increased that out of a total revenue of £1,200,000 some £500,000 came from beer!

The eighteenth century saw the beginnings of the breweries with names that are well-known today: Bass, Charrington, Coombe, Courage, Simmonds, Watney, Whitbread, Worthington. They offered their customers three beers, oddly enough all called ales, although hops were exclusively used for flavourings. They were pale ale, brown ale and old ale. In 1720 a London brewer produced a blend of all three which he called Entire. The market porters loved it and it became better known as Porter. It continued to be brewed for the next 250

years, but is now no longer available.

The nineteenth century was of particular importance, for scientific progress enabled brewing to become more efficient. After the publication of Pasteur's great work *Études sur la bière* (1857 on) beer also became more wholesome. Better hygiene and a proper understanding of the role of yeast removed many of the off-flavours that sometimes got into beer. Its keeping qualities were also improved. Towards the end of the century bottled beer appeared, home-brewed beer disappeared and even more revenue was raised.

An Act of 1880 made it illegal to brew beer at home without a licence, the cost of which was related to the rateable value of the property in which the beer was to be brewed. Furthermore, excise duty had to be paid on the beer in relation to its original gravity. The higher the gravity, and therefore the stronger the beer, the greater the tax. As a result brewing beer at home virtually ceased. Interest re-awakened after 1945 and in 1963 the relevant sections of the Act were repealed. The number of home-brewers increased considerably and today the activity is widespread throughout the community. It is now completely legal to brew your own beer without registration or taxation as long as you do not sell it.

The majority of home-brewers make their beer the easy way from prepared kits of malt extract containing hop oils and essence. Very palatable beers can be produced in this way with a minimum of trouble, and with a considerable saving compared with the price of commercial beers. Those who are a little more adventurous brew their own individual beers from a plain malt extract with hops and other adjuncts of their choice. This opens up a wide range of beers brewed to suit a personal palate. After some skill and experience has been acquired it is possible to select and mash assorted malts, other grains and adjuncts with water suitably adjusted and hops carefully selected. Such brewers are of the opinion that they are brewing true beers in the old tradition, but with the aid of modern technology.

BREWING BEER

Kits for making different styles of beer can nowadays be bought in a wide variety of outlets ranging from Boots and Woolworth in the High Street, to DIY centres, garden centres and, more especially, specialist home brew shops. The kits are of two kinds – wet and dry. The wet kit consists of a container full of toffee-like malt syrup mixed with hop flavouring. A sachet of dried beer yeast granules is usually attached to the label which gives step-by-step instructions for making the beer. The dry kit consists of a carton containing one sealed polythene bag of malt flour, and another of hops and grains. Sachets of dried beer yeast granules and finings are also supplied – again with full instructions. The kits are available in different sizes to brew from 16 to 40 pints of beer.

The styles include Bitter, Barley Wine, Stout, Brown Ale and Lager. Some kits are also marketed especially for diabetics. These produce a low carbohydrate beer but are relatively high in alcohol and so taste somewhat thin to many beer drinkers.

To make up a kit you need a large boiling pan and a fermentation bin. This can be the same kind of natural polythene bin used for making wine or just a large, but strong, polythene bag supported in a cardboard carton. A plastic stirring spoon is needed, together with a length of plastic tubing to siphon the beer into bottles. The latter must

be proper, strong beer bottles. It is dangerous to use any other kind in case they burst under pressure. If screw stoppers are not available for the bottles, crown caps and a crimping tool will be required.

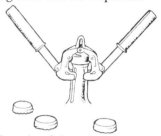

Hygiene is of the same importance to beer as it is to wine, mead and cider. All equipment must be clean and should be sterilised before use in the manner already described for making wine. Failure to observe this elementary advice is the cause of most of the off-flavours that are sometimes encountered.

Wet kits are usually made up by dissolving the malt syrup in hot water and boiling it for five minutes. Any additional sugar required is then stirred in and cold water is added to bring the quantity of wort up to the required level. When the temperature has fallen to 20°C (68°F), the yeast granules are sprinkled on, the brew stirred well and left to ferment out.

After five or six days, the brew is ready for bottling or casking.

Dry kits are made by boiling the hops and grains in water for about one hour and then straining the liquor into a bin containing the malt flour and additional sugar that have been mixed to a paste and then dissolved in warm water. Cold water is again used for topping up to the required quantity and when cool the yeast is added and well stirred in.

The manufacturers say that these beers are ready for drinking within a week of bottling or casking, but experience shows that they continue to improve for another two or three weeks. Several million people make these beers and seem well satisfied with the results. More individual beers can be made to suit your own palate, however, by using a plain malt extract to which you add adjuncts and hops of your own choice.

Malt extracts
Several manufacturers market plain malt syrups, as they are called, but prepared for different styles of beer.

Some of these are so prepared as to retain a quantity of diastase enzymes. They are called diastatic malt syrups, or DMS for short. These are particularly useful when you include adjuncts containing starch in your recipe. The diastase helps to convert the starch into a fermentable sugar.

You can, however, also use the malt extract usually given to delicate children, provided that it does not contain cod liver oil or the like!

Adjuncts
To a solution of the malt extract you can add other ingredients to vary the flavour and texture of the beer to suit your taste. These include flaked wheat, flaked rice, flaked maize, torrified barley, roasted barley, brewing flour, glucose chips, golden syrup, etc. etc., and hops of your choice.

Similar adjuncts can be used when you prepare your own malt solution direct from the barley grains. Before barley can be used for brewing it must first be treated by the maltster. In principle, he moistens and warms the grains until they begin to sprout. This releases the starch and the diastase enzymes that later convert the starch to maltose. Before this actually happens, however, he heats the grains to 50°C (122°F)

for a period so that they dry out and the enzymes are inhibited. This pale malt is the main source of sugar in the brewing of beer. By raising the temperature slightly, the maltster darkens the grains to form a crystal malt or, darker still, a chocolate malt and darkest of all a black malt. The latter bestows colour and flavour on a brew but no fermentable sugar.

Occasionally, untreated grains are lightly roasted and used to give a specific flavour to a beer. Other barley grains are so treated as to look like popcorn; this is called torrified barley.

Hops
The best hops are grown in Kent, Herefordshire and Worcestershire. As a result of research work at the Wye Agricultural Institute in Kent new varieties of hops have been developed from the popular Goldings and Fuggles. Goldings are used for the hardwater beers and Fuggles for the soft. The new varieties, respectively known as Wye Challenger and Wye Northdown, have a higher bittering potential and so slightly fewer of them are needed. Technology has also developed hop pellets that consist of only the essential part of the hops, the dross of leaf and stalk being discarded. Even fewer of these are needed. They are particularly useful to the home-brewer because they can be bought in sealed sachets that ensure their freshness. Furthermore, only two or three pellets per gallon need be added for dry hopping during fermentation. It is worth enquiring for these new varieties and experimenting with them.

FERMENTATION

Brewer's yeast is not often available to the home-brewer in a fresh form direct from a brewery and may well be contaminated if it is from a skimming. It is better to buy granulated brewer's yeast and to activate it in a cupful of tepid wort (40°C, 104°F) for fifteen minutes before use.

Twenty-four hours after fermentation starts the dirty froth should be skimmed from the surface of the beer and discarded. A clean tissue should then be used to wipe away the ring of dead yeast and other particles that will have collected on the side of the bin, level with the surface of the wort. Failure to do this can sometimes cause an unclean taste in the beer. The brew should then be thoroughly roused (stirred up) to admit air to the yeast and to enable it to reproduce a fresh colony of new cells. The cover should then be replaced on the bin.

Next day, this process should be repeated. By skimming off the surplus yeast, dead cells are discarded, avoiding a yeasty taste in the beer.

After the second skimming and stirring, dry hops, or hop pellets, may be added to impart a fresh tang to the beer. Hops are oily and very light. It is important, therefore, to wet them thoroughly. Squeeze them in the wort with your hand so that the thin petals absorb the liquor and sink to the bottom of the bin.

The brew can now be left, still covered, to finish fermenting for another three or four days. As far as possible maintain an even temperature between 17°C (63°F) and 20°C (68°F). The end of fermentation can be observed by the steady clearing of the froth and bubbles from the centre of the beer. The surface becomes clear and still.

At this point, move the bin to the coldest place you can find for a couple of days to encourage the solid particles in the beer to settle firmly on the bottom of the bin in the form of a thick paste. The beer is now ready for bottling or casking.

PRIMING

First remove a cupful of beer and dissolve in it the priming sugar at the rate of 20g (¾ oz) per gallon. Castor sugar dissolves more quickly than granulated sugar but either is adequate. Invert sugar or glucose may be used and an even better method is to reserve some 4% of the unfermented wort and use that for priming. In practical terms this is one pint out of three gallons of wort. It should be well sealed and stored in a refrigerator until required.

Absolute precision in the quantity of priming sugar used is not essential. However, too little will result in a flat or lifeless beer and too much will cause a great gush of foam when the bottle is opened. This will lift the secondary deposit and cloud the beer, spoiling both its appearance and taste. For those without scales, one level 5 ml spoonful of dry sugar per quart of beer is about right. Distribute the priming equally between the bottles. Alternatively, rack the beer from its deposit into a clean vessel, stir in the priming and then fill the bottles or cask. A 5 cm (2 in) gap should be left between the top of the beer and the bottom of the screw stopper or crown cap. Make sure that rubber washers or stoppers are clean, soft and in good condition, free from hardness and cracks. Sterilise both stoppers and caps before fitting them securely. The seal must be able to resist the pressure of the gas caused by the fermentation of the priming sugar, otherwise the beer will be flat when poured.

The rubber washer on the cap of the cask should be equally checked. The occasional smear of Vaseline helps to keep it soft and prevent it from sticking to the plastic keg. Screw it on as tightly as possible. Various types of casks are now available that contain

devices to maintain the pressure as the beer is drawn off through the tap. Others have facilities in the cap for the fitting of a CO_2 injector. When, say, half to two-thirds of the beer has been consumed, a squirt of carbon dioxide can be injected into the cask to maintain the pressure and keep the beer in good condition.

MATURING

Immediately after bottling or casking, the beer should be left in a temperature of 20°C (68°F) for four or five days to encourage the secondary fermentation. It should then be moved to a cool store to mature. The length of this period varies with the strength and body of the beer. One week is the minimum. Casked beer matures more quickly than bottled beer, which often needs three or four weeks and continues to improve for several months. All too often well-made beer is drunk before it is fully matured.

SERVING BEER

Americans and Continentals prefer to drink their beer much colder than Britons. Home-brewed beer should not be served so cold as to make it 'dumb', nor so warm as to cause it to pour with too much head that quickly disappears, leaving the beer lifeless. The range 10°–13°C (50°–55°F) seems to be the most suitable temperature, but you can experiment and choose a temperature most suitable to your own beer and preference.

Home-brewed beer looks best in a colourless short-stemmed glass, slightly incurved at the top. The colour and clarity, flecked with beads of bubbles, please the eye, the foamy head is held in the narrowing mouth and emits the bouquet of the malt and hops. Glass mugs have a little less aesthetic appearance, but this is offset by the handle that enables you to hold it without masking the beer within. Silver, pewter and earthenware mugs may keep the beer cool for longer, but eye appeal is lost and who wants to keep their beer that long?

Beer tastes good on its own and even better with cold meats, cheese and strong-flavoured salads like onions, radishes, watercress and celery. With good crusty bread and butter, or baked jacket potato you have a well-balanced and nutritious meal.

DEXTRIN

During the mashing of malt grains, substances collectively called dextrin are released. The higher the mashing temperature the greater the quantity of dextrin produced. Even a few degrees fahrenheit make a difference. Dextrin, although a sugar, is not readily fermentable and often remains in a beer to give it body and a less dry taste.

When fermentation is finished, some dextrin often remains and a specific gravity test may reveal a reading of up to 1.008. Provided the beer has completely finished fermenting and is absolutely still and without trace of bubbles, it is safe to bottle the beer and prime it as described. Beer should not be bottled above this figure in case there is too great a secondary fermentation producing an excess of carbon dioxide. The original gravities given in the recipes refer to the fermentable sugars among the ingredients because the gravity of the dextrins cannot be deduced owing to individual variations in the quality of the ingredients and the way they are mashed. Accordingly, a specific gravity reading in excess of that given may be recorded before fermentation begins and may be equally in excess of 1.000 when the fermentation ends.

RECIPES

Some recipes are given for making beer from malt extract and adjuncts, and others for mashing the grains with adjuncts. Even so, you will want to experiment for yourself. Accordingly, the following guidelines are set out to save you from spoiling a brew.
1 When 450g (1 lb) of granulated household white sugar is dissolved in water and made

107

up to 4.5 litres (1 gallon), a specific gravity of 1.036 is achieved. It is important to remember that in all recipes that 450g (1 lb) sugar occupies half a pint of volume. Thus, 450g (1 lb) sugar dissolved in 4.25 litres (7½ pints) of water makes a total of 4.5 litres (8 pints).

2 When 450g (1 lb) of the toffee-like malt syrup is dissolved in water and made up to 4.5 litres (1 gallon), a specific gravity of around 1.028 should be achieved. Minor variations depend on the manufacturer. It is rarely necessary to use more than 450g (1 lb) of malt syrup in the making of 4.5 litres (1 gallon) of beer.

3 Pale malt should always form the main basis of your grain mashed beers; 450g (1 lb) pale malt grains mashed to end point in 4.5 litres (1 gallon) of water will produce a specific gravity of about 1.024. Theoretically, 1.027 should be achieved, but it rarely is in the home. Most beers have an original gravity between 1.030 and 1.050, so this gives you a guide as to how much pale malt to use.

4 The quantity of sugar used should never produce more than one-third of the alcohol, and preferably no more than one-quarter. The beer otherwise becomes unbalanced and thin.

5 The quantity of adjuncts used should never consist of more than one-fifth of the malt and preferably only one-tenth.

6 Hard water is needed for all bitter type beers and barley wines. Soft water is needed for stouts, brown ales and lagers. If chlorine is known to be in your tap water, then all the water you use for brewing should be boiled for at least one minute in an open pan. Otherwise your beer may taste of TCP!

7 The savings in tax, overheads and labour are so great in home-brewing that it is a waste of money ever to use less than the best-quality ingredients. Poor goods inevitably make poor beer.

Easy bitter (OG 1.040)

Malt extract	900g	2 lb
Sugar	340g	12 oz
Golding hops	50g	1¾ oz
Water	9 l	2 gal
Beer yeast		

Dissolve the malt extract in a quart of the warmed water, rinsing out the container to ensure that none is wasted.

Boil the hops in two quarts of water for 20 minutes, then strain on to the malt solution.

Add two more quarts of water to the hops, boil them again for a further 20 minutes, then strain on to the malt. Discard the hops to the rose garden.

Stir in the sugar and add the rest of the water (cold) and leave the wort to cool down to 20°C (68°F).

Stir in the activated yeast, then skim, stir, bottle and prime as already described.

Easy brown (OG 1.032)

Malt extract	900g	2 lb
Black malt	55g	2 oz
Brown sugar	125g	4½ oz
Fuggles hops	30g	1 oz
Water	9 l	2 gal
Pinch of salt		
Beer yeast		

Dissolve the malt extract, sugar and salt in half a gallon of the warmed water, add the black malt and hops, wetting them thoroughly, and boil for half an hour. Leave for five minutes then strain into a bin and rinse the hops with a pint of hot water, before discarding them.

Add the rest of the water (cold) and, when the temperature of the wort has fallen to 20°C (68°F), mix in activated yeast.

Skim, stir and prime as already described. This is a dry beer. It can be marginally sweetened with 125g (4½ oz) lactose.

Easy stout (OG 1.044)

Malt extract	900g	2 lb
Crystal malt grains	250g	9 oz
Black malt	125g	4½ oz
Brown sugar	250g	9 oz
Fuggle's hops	50g	1¾ oz

Water	9 l	2 gal
Pinch of salt		
Stout yeast		

Dissolve the malt extract in half a gallon of the warmed water, stir in the crushed crystal malt and the whole black malt. Add three-quarters of the hops, wetting them thoroughly, and the pinch of salt. Bring to the boil and maintain a steady roll for 45 minutes. Add the rest of the hops and boil for a further 15 minutes.

Leave to cool for 15 minutes then strain out the solids and discard them. Stir in the sugar, add the rest of the water (cold) and when the temperature has fallen to 20°C (68°F) add the activated yeast.

Skim, stir and prime as already described (p. 106).

Strong ale (OG 1.056)

Malt extract DMS	1.8 kg	4 lb
Golding hops	70g	2½ oz
Water	8 l	14 pt
Beer yeast		

Boil the hops in 4 litres (7 pints) of the water for 45 minutes keeping the pan covered and maintaining a rolling boil. Leave for 5 minutes to allow the hops to settle, then strain the liquor into a bin and discard the hops.

Stir in the malt extract and make sure that it is completely dissolved. Add cold water to the 9 litres (2 gallon) level and when cool (20°C/68°F) mix in the activated yeast. Continue as already described (p. 106). Mature this beer for 3 months.

Light ale (OG 1.034)

Malt extract (DMS)	450g	1 lb
Pale malt grains	250g	9 oz
Flaked rice	200g	7 oz
Sugar	250g	9 oz
Challenger hops	28g	1 oz
Hard water	9 l	2 gal
Beer yeast		

Heat half the water to 70°C (157°F), stir in the malt extract, crushed pale malt grains

and flaked rice. Cover the vessel and maintain a temperature of 65.5°C (150°F) for one hour.

Add the hops, wetting them thoroughly and boil the wort for half an hour. Leave to cool for five minutes, then strain out the solids, stir in the sugar and add the rest of the water. Leave to cool to 20°C (68°F), then mix in the activated yeast.

Continue as already described (p. 106).

Bitter beer (OG 1.040)

Malt extract (DMS)	450g	1 lb
Pale malt grains	400g	14 oz
Crystal malt grains	100g	3½ oz
Flaked maize	200g	7 oz
Roasted barley	200g	7 oz
Sugar	250g	9 oz
Challenger hops	35g	1¼ oz
Hard water	9 l	2 gal
Beer yeast		

Heat half the water to 70°C (157°F), stir in the malt extract, the crushed pale malt and crystal malt, the flaked maize and roasted barley. Maintain a temperature of 66.5°C (152°F) for one hour.

Add three-quarters of the hops and boil the wort for half an hour, then add the remainder and continue to boil for a further fifteen minutes. Leave to cool for five minutes, then strain out the hops and grains, stir in the sugar, add the remaining cold water and leave to cool. At 20°C (68°F), add the activated yeast and continue as already described (p. 106).

Pale ale (OG 1.036)

Malt extract (DMS)	450g	1 lb
Pale malt grains	250g	9 oz
Flaked rice	200g	7 oz
Sugar	250g	9 oz
Challenger hops	28g	1 oz
Hard water	9 l	2 gal
Beer yeast		

Heat half the water to 70°C (157°F), stir in the malt extract, the crushed pale malt grains and flaked rice. Cover and leave for one hour, maintaining a temperature of 65.5°C (150°F).

Add the hops, boil for half an hour, leave for five minutes, then strain out and discard the solids. Stir in the sugar, add the remaining cold water and, when cool, the activated yeast. Continue as already described (p. 106).

Export ale (OG 1.050)

Malt extract (DMS)	450g	1 lb
Crystal malt grains	100g	3½ oz
Pale malt grains	500g	18 oz
Flaked maize	250g	9 oz
Flaked wheat	65g	2¼ oz
Sugar	400g	14 oz
Challenger hops (Golding)	40g	1½ oz
Hard water	9 l	2 gal
Beer yeast		

Heat half the water to 70°C (157°F), stir in the malt extract, the crystal malt, the crushed pale malt, flaked maize and flaked wheat. Cover and leave for one hour, maintaining a temperature of 66.5°C (152°F).

Add all but a handful of hops and boil for one hour. Leave for five minutes then strain out and discard all the solids, stir in the sugar, add the rest of the water and leave until cool. Add the activated yeast and ferment as described on p. 106. Mix in the remaining hops after the second skimming.

Brown ale (OG 1.030)

Malt extract (DMS)	450g	1 lb
Crystal malt grains	250g	9 oz
Brown sugar	400g	14 oz
Northdown (Fuggle) hops	28g	1 oz
Lactose	100g	3½ oz
Soft water	9 l	2 gal
Beer yeast		

Heat half the water to 70°C (157°F), stir in the malt extract, the crushed crystal malt grains, cover and maintain a temperature of 64.5°C (148°F), for half an hour. Add the hops and boil for half an hour. Leave for five

minutes then strain out the hops and grains and stir in the sugar and lactose. Add the rest of the soft cold water and, when cool enough, the activated yeast. Continue as described on p.106.

The beer will finish with a slightly sweet taste. If a dry brown ale is required omit the lactose.

Irish-style stout (OG 1.042)

Malt extract (DMS)	450g	1 lb
Pale malt grains	450g	1 lb
Crystal malt grains	250g	9 oz
Black malt grains	100g	3½ oz
Roasted barley	100g	3½ oz
Brewing flour	100g	3½ oz
Brown sugar	250g	9 oz
Northdown (Fuggle) Hops	40g	1½ oz
Soft water	9 l	2 gal
Stout yeast		

Heat the malt extract, pale malt, crystal malt, black malt, roasted barley and brewing flour at 64.5°C (148°F) for one hour. Add all but a handful of hops and boil for 45 minutes. Leave for five minutes. Strain out the solids, stir in the sugar. Continue as described on p. 106. Dry hop after second skimming.

15 Everyone has problems sometimes

Problems are easier to prevent than to cure. The use of sensible and good-quality ingredients, proper attention to hygiene and sound methods are the secrets of success. Avoid unusual, damaged, mouldy or stale ingredients and clean all ingredients before use. Sterilise all equipment before use. Rack all fermented beverages from their lees as soon as fermentation has finished and again as soon as a further deposit can be seen. Keep jars and bottles full and well-sealed, except for sherry-style wine. Follow these simple guidelines and you will have few problems. Even so, you may occasionally encounter one of the following difficulties over the years.

Absence of bouquet
Most likely due to lack of acid during fermentation. Poor-quality ingredients could be a contributory factor. If the beverage is otherwise sound, blend it with a more strongly flavoured one.

Bad-egg smell
Not very common. Some yeasts produce hydrogen sulphide, but the lack of vitamin B_1 in the ingredients is the most likely cause. The inclusion of some grape in one form or another, or a Benerva tablet, prevents the problem. There is no known cure.

Bitter almond smell and taste
This is caused by the inclusion of fruit stones or kernels, or broken pips. Prevention is obvious but there is no cure.

Flowers of wine
This is a thin skin of white fungus known as *Mycoderma vini*, that develops on alcoholic beverages exposed to the air – even through an ill-fitting or loose cork or stopper. The remedy is to float off the powdery fungus and to sterilise the beverage with sulphite at the rate of 100 ppm.

Geranium smell
This only develops when potassium sorbate is used without the addition of a Campden tablet. Again, easily preventable but impossible to cure.

Hazes
Fairly common and mostly curable, but first check the cause of the haze. When fermentation finishes, the wine, mead, cider or beer should begin to clear from the top downwards and a deposit should begin to build up on the bottom of the container. After the first racking, and removal to a cold store, the beverage should clear to brightness naturally within a month or two. Sometimes, however, minute particles of debris remain in suspension. They probably consist of yeast cells, pulp, protein, tannin and so on, but may be due to pectin from fruits, starch from root vegetables and grain, or from contamination with a metal other than stainless steel.

General debris can be removed with a proprietary brand of fining gell or with isinglass or bentonite. Follow the instructions on the packet regarding the quantity to use and the method of mixing it into the hazy beverage. Leave the container in as cold a place as you can for a week by which time the haze should have deposited. Rack the clear wine into a sterilised container, seal and store.

If the haze does not clear, test for pectin (if fruit was used), or starch (if vegetables or grain were used). A teaspoonful of the beverage mixed into and thoroughly shaken up with two tablespoonfuls of methylated spirits will show up pectin as small clots or strings within an hour. The remedy is to mix in an appropriate measure of a pectolytic enzyme and leave the container in a warm place for 24 hours and then in a cold store for a few days. The clear wine should then be racked off.

A starch haze can be detected by placing a tablespoonful of the beverage in a white saucer and adding one or two drops of household tincture of iodine as used for cuts and scratches. If the beverage turns blue, or darkens, then starch is present. The remedy is fungal amylase used in accordance with the manufacturer's instructions.

A metallic haze is most easily detected by smell and taste. The remedy is too dangerous for use in the home and the beverage should be discarded. Fortunately the risk of metallic haze is extremely rare, and can easily be avoided by not using any metal equipment, unless it is stainless steel.

Filtration is rarely necessary, but should you decide to use a filter to polish the wine for a competition, allow plenty of time for the wine to recover and don't forget to use sulphite to avoid excessive oxidation.

Insipid taste
This is undoubtedly due to insufficient acid. Try dissolving a teaspoonful of acid in some of the wine and mix it into the rest. Alternatively, blend the wine with one that is too sharp, perhaps a rhubarb or a blackcurrant wine.

Mousiness
A smell and taste reminiscent of mice some-times develops in beverages that contain too little acid and have not been sulphited. Cause is due to infection by bacteria and there is no remedy. Discard the beverage and sterilise all containers. In slightly affected beverages, many people are unable to detect this odour.

Oxidation
If a beverage is allowed to come into contact with air, it absorbs the oxygen and develops a dull, flat taste. Occasionally, it has been cured by refermenting the beverage. It is easier to prevent oxidation by keeping vessels full and well covered at all times.

Ropiness
A not very common disease caused by lacto bacteria that form slimy ropes. The beverage has an oily sheen and pours slightly thick. Beat the beverage with a plastic spoon to break up the ropes and add sulphite at the rate of 100 ppm. Leave it in a cold place and after a few days rack the now normal bever-age into a sterilised container.

Rotting vegetation
An odour and taste of rotting cabbage leaves is sometimes found in a beverage that has not been racked from its lees. It is caused by the decomposition of fruit pulp and dead yeast cells. There is no known cure, but preven-tion is so easy that it should never occur in your beverages.

Sulphur
An overdose of sulphite and Campden tab-lets in solution can cause a sulphuric odour. It soon disappears and no harm is done. Keep the Campden tablets down to no more than two per gallon (100 ppm). Some people are more sensitive than others to this odour.

Vinegar smell and/or taste
Acetic acid is sometimes formed during fermentation. It can also develop in unsul-phited wines made from fruit infected with *Mycoderma aceti* and in other alcoholic liquids inadequately covered. Beverages that are

only slightly affected can be sulphited at the rate of 100 ppm, and may be used in cooking. Badly affected wine, beer, mead or cider may be turned into vinegar and used as such. Otherwise, discard and sterilise.

Yeast bite
A bitter taste sometimes found in beers and caused by fermenting at too high a temperature and not removing dead yeast cells on the fermentation vessel. No known cure. Discard if too severe.

Appendices

HYDROMETER TABLES

Specific gravity	Sugar in 1 gallon / 4.5 litres		Alchohol equivalent Possible / Probable	
	oz	g	%	%
1.005	2	57	0.71	0.6
1.010	4	113	1.39	1.3
1.015	6	170	2.05	1.9
1.020	8	226	2.71	2.5
1.025	10	283	3.42	3.1
1.030	12½	354	4.08	3.8
1.035	14½	410	4.75	4.4
1.040	16½	467	5.44	5.0
1.045	18½	525	6.13	5.6
1.050	21	596	6.79	6.3
1.055	23	653	7.47	6.9
1.060	25	709	8.18	7.5
1.065	27	765	8.84	8.1
1.070	29	822	9.53	8.8
1.075	31	879	10.19	9.4
1.080	33	936	10.89	10.0
1.085	35½	1008	11.61	10.6
1.090	37½	1065	12.31	11.3
1.095	40	1135	12.92	11.9
1.100	42	1188	13.54	12.5
1.105	44	1248	14.24	13.1
1.110	46	1305	14.98	13.8
1.115	48	1362	15.62	14.4
1.120	50	1419	15.32	15.0
1.125	52	1475	17.01	15.6
1.130	54	1532	17.71	16.3
1.135	56	1588	18.41	16.9

Note 2 lb sugar dissolved in a liquid occupies 1 pint of volume. 1 kg sugar dissolved in a liquid occupies 620 mls of volume.

The potential percentage of alcohol is by volume and assumes that 47.5% of the sugar is converted to alcohol. In practice this is almost impossible to achieve and probable percentage is the more likely figure to be achieved in the home. However, this figure assumes that all the sugar will be converted to alcohol, carbon dioxide, glycerine, the acids and other by-products of the fermentation.

When taking a hydrometer reading of a must prior to fermentation it should be remembered that the figure will be distorted by the presence of acids, tannin and soluble pulp debris, and will not precisely record only the fermentable sugar content. An allowance of up to 4 units should be made if you are seeking as much accuracy as possible.

When taking a hydrometer reading of a must that has finished fermenting, it should be remembered that alcohol is lighter than water. A reading of 1.000, for example, does not imply complete dryness since the alcohol formed will have diluted the wine. A completely dry wine without residual sugar is likely to have a specific gravity of between 0.990 and 0.994, depending on the strength of the wine.

However, for most home winemakers and brewers it is adequate to take the figures as they are for the presence or absence of half a percent of alcohol by volume is unlikely to be noticeable, even to an experienced palate.

COMPARATIVE WEIGHTS

Metric		British/USA	Metric		British/USA
28.35g	1	0.035 oz	0.45 kg	1	2.20 lb
56.70g	2	0.07 oz	0.91 kg	2	4.41 lb
85.05g	3	0.115 oz	1.36 kg	3	6.6 lb
113.40g	4	0.14 oz	1.81 kg	4	8.82 lb
141.75g	5	0.175 oz	2.27 kg	5	11.02 lb
170.10g	6	0.21 oz	2.72 kg	6	13.23 lb
198.45g	7	0.245 oz	3.18 kg	7	15.43 lb
226.80g	8	0.28 oz	3.63 kg	8	17.64 lb
255.15g	9	0.31 oz	4.08 kg	9	19.84 lb
283.50g	10	0.35 oz	4.50 kg	10	22.00 lb

Centre figures can be read either metric or British/USA e.g. 1 kg = 2.20 lbs or 1 lb = 0.45 kg.

COMPARATIVE TEMPERATURES

Centigrade	Fahrenheit	Centigrade	Fahrenheit
0	32	55	131
5	41	60	140
10	50	65	149
15	59	70	158
20	68	75	167
25	77	80	176
30	86	85	185
35	95	90	194
40	104	95	203
45	113	100	212
50	122		

10°C Suitable temperature for serving cold cups, white and rosé table wines, sparkling wines. Also for fermenting lager-type beer.
20°C Suitable temperature for serving red table wines, dessert wines and liqueurs. Also for fermenting wines and beers.
60°C Suitable temperature for serving mulled wines.
65–70°C Suitable temperatures for mashing malted grains for beer.

COMPARATIVE LIQUID MEASURES

British	Metric	American
1 gallon (8 pints)	4.56 litres	10 pints
1 pint (20 fl oz)	0.57 litres	1¼ pints
1 fl oz	28 mls	1 fl oz
1 tablespoon (⅝ fl oz)	15 mls	⅓ fl oz
1 dessertspoon (⅓ fl oz)	5 mls	1 tablespoon
1 teaspoon (⅙ fl oz)	5 mls	⅐ fl oz

American	Metric	British
1 gallon (8 pints)	3.8 litres	6⅔ pints
1 pint (16 fl oz)	.475 litres	⅘ pint
1 cup (8 fl oz)	.237 litres	⅖ pint
1 tablespoon (⅓ fl oz)	10 mls	⅓ fl oz (1 dessertspoon)
1 teaspoon (⅐ fl oz)	4 mls	⅘ teaspoon

Metric	British	American
5 mls	⅙ fl oz (teaspoon)	⅐ fl oz
10 mls	⅓ fl oz (dessertspoon)	⅓ fl oz (tablespoon)
¼ litre	8¾ fl oz	8½ lb
½ litre	17½ fl oz	1 pint + 4 tablespoons
¾ litre	1⅓ pints	1 pint 10 fl oz
1 litre	1¾ pints	2 pints + 8 tablespoons

THE ACIDITY OF POPULAR FRUITS

Fruit	Dominant acid	Degree
Blackcurrant	Citric	
Redcurrant	Citric	
Whitecurrant	Citric	Very high
Damson	Malic	
Lemon	Citric	
Cherry (cooking)	Malic	
Gooseberry	Citric/Malic (equal)	High to very high
Greengage	Malic	
Rhubarb	Malic	
Apricot	Malic	
Plum	Malic	High
Raspberry	Citric	
Apple (cooking)	Malic	
Blackberry	Citric/Malic (equal)	
Grape	Tartaric	
Pineapple	Citric	Medium to high
Quince	Malic	
Strawberry	Citric	
Bilberry	Citric	
Elderberry	Citric	Medium
Orange	Citric	
Apple (eating)	Malic	
Cherry (eating)	Malic	
Mulberry	Citric	Low to medium
Peach	Malic	
Raisins and Sultanas	Tartaric	
Banana	Malic	Very low
Pear	Malic	

Index

Index